The COST
OF LIVING

The COST OF LIVING

A
Personal
Journey
into John's
Gospel

MARGARET CUNDIFF

UPPER
ROOM BOOKS®
NASHVILLE

Original edition published by The Bible Reading Fellowship, Oxford, England.
E-mail: inquiries@brf.org.uk Web site: http://www.brf.org.uk

The Upper Room® Web site: http://www.upperroom.org

UPPER ROOM®, UPPER ROOM BOOKS® and design logos are trademarks
owned by The Upper Room®, Nashville, Tennessee. All rights reserved.

Cover & interior design: Gore Studio Inc.
Cover art: "Man on Tightrope" by David Douglas
First Printing: 2002

Library of Congress Cataloging-in-Publication Data
Cundiff, Margaret.
        The cost of living : a personal journey into John's gospel / by Margaret Cundiff.
              p. cm.
        Originally published: London : Triangle, 1987.
        ISBN 0-8358-0960-9
              1. Bible. N.T. John XI-XXI--Criticism, interpretation, etc. 2. Chris-
tian life. 3. Cundiff, Margaret. I. Title.

BS2615.2 .C87 2002
226.5'06—dc21   2001045441

Printed in the United States of America

FOR PETER,
*with love and thanks
as we celebrate
our forty years of marriage*

Contents —⌒

By way of explanation ⟶

WHY DID I CHOOSE to write about these chapters from John's Gospel—chapters 11 to 21, the second half of the Gospel? They portray so vividly the cost of living the Jesus way of life. Jesus raises his friend to life and starts on the road to Calvary, which for him is death, then life. The road he takes is the road we must take, toward our own death; and, if we will accept Jesus' gift, it is the road to life for us as well.

These chapters are, for me, exciting, compelling, demanding. But there are two difficulties. Unlike the Gospel of Mark, which is very plain, direct reading that almost anyone can understand (and that is why it is so often chosen to give to new Christians), John's Gospel has within it great theological argument, which is all of a piece with the narrative. So those with little background of Christian teaching may read about the events but miss out on the deep truths that are so vital for them. On the other hand, for Christians who know their Bibles, the words are so familiar that these readers too are in danger of missing the deeper meaning.

I am trying to meet both groups. I want those who know these chapters well to look at them in the light of the world we live in, the harsh realities at the beginning of the twenty-first century. I want those who are almost totally caught up with today's world and its problems to turn and look at Jesus and walk the road with him to death and to life. I want us all to meet the characters, hear the debates, witness the natural and supernatural events, and not to be afraid of those who say, "Oh yes, but there's more to it than that!"

I like to think I am traveling the road with both groups, adding my comments, sharing how I feel and how certain situations remind me of my own experience, being forced to forget my preconceived ideas and be open to what Jesus has to say to me on the road.

So who is the book for? Anyone who is willing to walk with me! I hope that what I write will be from the heart as well as from the head, and will remind me that I have to make up my own mind about the issues of life and death. I have to be willing to see things in a new light, and I may have to alter my views on some things. I find it exciting—I hope others will too.

As you are reading this book, you will find it helpful to read also the relevant passages from John's Gospel. I have given the appropriate reference at the head of each of my chapters.

—*Margaret Cundiff*

Chapter 1

Point of no return

John 11:1-16

THERE ARE EVENTS in our lives which, when we look back at them, we can see were both ends and beginnings. Each was a moment of decision, which affected every other moment from then on—a small step, as it seemed at the time, leaving behind all that had gone before and putting the seal on all that was to come. It may have been the way we answered a question or responded to someone's need. It could have been an action taken on the spur of the moment or, after agonizing thought and discussion, in emotional response or as a result of calculating the pros and cons of that certain course.

When did Jesus take the step that made the cross inevitable? At what stage in his life did he "burn his bridges"? You could say that in one way there was never a choice at all; but to say that is to deny the reality of free will, the gift of the Father to his Son as much as to us. Without free will we would be robots, mere puppets on strings, responding only to the tugs and whims of the Heavenly Controller, dancing to his tune, incapable of personal response. God the Father gave to Jesus his Son, his heir of earth and heaven, freedom of the universe. Jesus came to this earth as a baby yet with the status of Lord. He "came of age" when he came to earth. He was free to decide, to act, and to reap the result.

There are many ways to choose from, many paths to follow, yet in the final analysis only two: the way of life or the way of death . . . but life or death for whom?

Jesus was always in danger, a fugitive. From his birth he was on the run. His parents had to carry him as a babe in arms away to Egypt for safety. Herod, in anger and fear, had his squad of butchers murder all the baby boys two years of age and under in the Bethlehem area because the infant Jesus was a threat to his plans, and Jesus continued to be a threat to those who would use power and prestige for their own ends. Time after time Jesus escaped by the skin of his teeth—or by the grace of God—from the hands of violent people. Many perceived him as a threat as long as he was alive; the only way they saw to contain Jesus was by destroying him, removing him from the scene.

Yet there were times of peace and security for Jesus. Times when, away from those who aimed to destroy him, he was sought out by those who looked for the secret of life, of health, of peace. These were ordinary people for the most part, called "common" people—because there were so many of them! They were those who had open minds and open hearts.

So we see Jesus, having escaped from the dangers of Jerusalem across the River Jordan, enjoying a period of successful ministry— preaching, teaching, and healing. People were responding to him. Many of them had been prepared by John the Baptist and were ready in heart and mind for Jesus, in whom they recognized the one whom John had promised. Some may have witnessed the baptism of Jesus by John. They accepted Jesus with love.

Success at last! A growing support, a safe haven—things were looking up! Then a message arrived for Jesus. It was a simple message, sent from friends of his, two sisters who loved him and who looked to him in their need now. Their brother, Lazarus, was desperately ill. No one could help him—no one except, as the sisters Mary and Martha knew, their family friend Jesus. Yet he was much more than a family friend. He was the Lord and Master, for the message was "Lord, he whom you love is ill." Just that. No demands, no suggestion as to what Jesus should do, how he should respond, just the facts of the situation. Maybe they did not ask him to come because they knew that coming would put him in danger. Perhaps they did not ask because they knew that distance made no difference to his love and power. They just put the facts before him.

What options did Jesus have? To rush immediately to Bethany, responding as fast as possible. To ask his Father to heal Lazarus—after all, he did not have to be physically present at the bedside of Lazarus to heal him. He had no need to put himself in danger by going to see Lazarus. He could have sent a messenger with words of sympathy for the sisters. Or he could have decided that his place was with the people who were responding to his message where he already was. After all, what was one person's need compared with the needs of the crowd?

He did . . . nothing. He talked about the result of the illness not being final—meaning death. He spoke of what had happened as bringing glory to God and also of its being the means of his glory; but he did nothing. For two days he did nothing. No message, no action—nothing.

Have you ever waited for two days for something to happen? For a letter, a phone call, a visit? Have you ever sat by the bedside of someone very ill for two days, when nothing seemed to happen one way or the other? Have you ever suffered pain, loneliness, depression, anxiety, fear, or anything else for two days? Two days can seem like a lifetime. Two days when nothing happens are an eternity, when heaven and earth stand still, when we are suspended out of time, out of life.

What was Jesus thinking about for two days? What were his friends thinking about—those who had heard the message? And what about the messenger?

Then Jesus announced his decision—"Let us go to Judea again." He would go to his friend Lazarus. He would go, as he said, "to awake him." He was going in his own time, the right time.

In the Old Testament, the book of Ecclesiastes (which means "The Preacher") describes in very poetic language that everything has its right time.

> For everything there is a season,
> and a time for every matter under heaven:
> a time to be born, and a time to die;

a time to plant, and a time to pluck up what is planted;
a time to kill, and a time to heal;
a time to break down, and a time to build up;
a time to weep, and a time to laugh;
a time to mourn, and a time to dance;
a time to throw away stones, and a time to gather stones together;
a time to embrace, and a time to refrain from embracing;
a time to seek, and a time to lose;
a time to keep, and a time to throw away;
a time to tear, and a time to sew;
a time to keep silence, and a time to speak;
a time to love, and a time to hate;
a time for war, and a time for peace. (Eccles. 3:1-8)

Yes, there is "the right time" for everything. This was plain in the ministry of Jesus. He sought his Father's time, the perfect time.

We want things in our time, and that time is usually "now"— for we live in a world that knows only "now." Ours is a society of instant coffee and the instant answer; a microwave society, which has satisfaction on demand, done just right. Almost as the thought enters the head, it is expected in the hand. So when, instead of an immediate answer to our prayers, we hear only the sound of our own voice, we either panic, shout and scream, jump up and down like demented figures on space-invader games, or we arrogantly pronounce judgment: "There is no God, there is no answer; we have proved it so."

Our lives are governed by time, our time—the days, the hours, the minutes, the seconds. We surround ourselves with reminders of time. No public building is complete without its intrusive clock face, no wrist so small that an expression of the passing of time cannot be strapped to it. And in case we fail to give due deference to the passage of time, we are reminded by alarms—strident, loud, or a tinkling tune—all saying, "You must do it, have it, experience it *now*, for time is passing."

Jesus took his time, because he waited for the right time in God's economy. He took time to listen to God, while he got on with what needed doing. During the two days of waiting, he would discover what was to come. The way to glory was open, and that way was through death to life.

When Jesus made his decision and told his disciples, they tried to dissuade him. They knew that it spelled danger. When he asked them to go with him, I imagine there were murmurings, fear for their own skins, for they knew it was likely that whatever would befall Jesus would be their fate also. Thomas, the one we malign as the doubter, faced up to the fact of the situation, and took the lead with courage: "Let us also go, that we may die with him." Thomas was prepared to give everything, even life itself, to be with Jesus. Was he scared? Did he really realize how desperate the situation was? I believe he was and did, for Thomas was a down-to-earth facer of facts; and so his courage was even greater, for he knew the odds and accepted them. What really mattered was being with Jesus; that outweighed comfort or safety.

None of us likes putting our head into a noose. Most of us would choose a life of calm, secure contentment. Oh yes, we want to be stimulated, excited, enriched by life—but within safe bounds. Our life is very precious. It is to be guarded, for we have only the one life and therefore we must make the most of it and use it to its full extent. We all have a built-in defense mechanism, a self-preservation instinct. And yet in certain circumstances something or someone else can transcend those restrictions. We can "live dangerously." It will be because of love—love for a child, for a friend, for country; that love Jesus describes as totally self-giving. The fear of death can be outweighed by the power of love, and the fact of death freely accepted as the cost of living.

No barrier can withstand love. Jesus and his friends were now on their way to prove that fact for all time.

Chapter 2 ⟶

"Too late, too late" was the cry

John 11:17-37

WHEN DEATH OR TRAGEDY OCCURS, life for those closest—
the family, friends—goes into reverse. Each moment, each
event, is analyzed, almost as though doing so can reverse the irre-
versible. The words I hear most frequently as I visit a bereaved family are "If only . . . ." I see in their faces sorrow over what might have
been. Death has come down like a curtain, blotting out signs of the
future. There seems only one way to look—back. The past comes
tumbling back with its missed opportunities and wrong turns. It is
then that blame is apportioned; guilt rises; and accusations are made.

I have sat in homes where, although not a word has been spoken, I have felt the atmosphere of regret, guilt, and accusation.
These feelings are natural reactions, although people often are
ashamed to feel them and so keep them bottled up. People are
much better off when they bring such feelings out into the open,
express them and deal with them rather than allowing them to
become festering wounds and a blight on the future.

Martha and Mary sent the message to Jesus that his friend,
their brother, Lazarus, was ill. They confidently expected that Jesus
would help them and that their brother would recover. What did
they feel as they saw Lazarus grow steadily worse, until the battle
for life was lost? Then there followed the elaborate ceremonies,
the burial and the mourning, all according to custom. Friends and
neighbors came to share this time, to pay their respects, and to be
with the sisters—but not Jesus.

At last, four days after the funeral, Jesus appeared—too late,
much too late. Too late to help Lazarus, too late to be at the burial,

too late to be of any assistance. The one person the sisters had wanted to be there was too late. How did they feel when they heard that Jesus was almost at the door? Martha went out to meet him; Mary stayed in the house. Did Mary stay in because she could not bring herself to face Jesus, to speak of her brother's death? Was she disappointed in him? Was she angry with him? How many times did she say and think, "If only . . ."?

Martha met Jesus with those words: "Lord, if you had been here, my brother would not have died." She believed in her Lord who healed the sick, but could she believe in a Lord who raised the dead? She believed that Jesus was in a special relationship with God, and so the impossible was possible, but how that was to be, she did not know. She could only cry out with faith in the orthodox Jewish belief in life after death, unknown and shadowy but real: "I know that he will rise again in the resurrection on the last day."

Martha's faith was like the mustard seed, so small and simple, yet containing the germ of life and potential for growth. Jesus responded with those words that still bring comfort and hope to mourners in a present-day funeral home, with its canned hymns and plastic flowers, as much as to that grieving country girl who stood before him: "I am the resurrection and the life." That girl could only look into his eyes and answer with confidence his question, "Do you believe this?" for she knew him as a friend. She knew him personally; she knew, too, that he was the Messiah, the Son of God, the one for whom her people the Jews had looked for all those centuries.

I look into the faces of the mourners when I conduct a funeral. Sometimes the church is crowded with friends and relations, there to pay their last respects. Other times there may be just one surviving relative by the graveside of an elderly person. When the death has been sudden or a young person has died, the church or funeral home is filled with young people, who perhaps had never given death a thought until a car crash or disease, raging like a forest fire, snatched the life of one of their friends. I see grief, despair, fear, anger. They look at me, searching for an answer, hoping for some light, and whatever the circumstances, I can look back at them and say, "Jesus says: 'I am the resurrection and the life.'"

Do they believe me? Some do, some don't. Their faces give me their answer. Sometimes I realize that they pity me for believing the words I say. But often I see the answer "I do believe," and I know that they will be able to cope, to come to terms with death, because they know that death is not the end, because they trust in the promise of Jesus. They have something to hold on to, a future to look forward to.

Martha knew that assurance in her grief, and her first thought was to share it with her sister, Mary. Because she knew that Mary would want to hear it from Jesus himself, she lovingly took the initiative and gave her sister the message that Jesus wanted to see her. She wanted Mary to have time with him alone so that he could give her the comfort and assurance she needed to face what was to come.

In our anxiousness to help the bereaved, we talk too much. It is a natural reaction: we think we are helping them by not allowing them to be alone, to brood, to cry, to remember. The bereaved are given sleeping pills to "get them through the night," to keep them from thinking about what has happened. And yet what they do need is time—time when they can unburden their hearts before God, time to question God, to be angry, to cry, to complain, and to allow God to meet with them.

When I visit the bereaved, I just listen to them, allow them to tell me all that they want to say, and then I give them space. I leave a card that has verses from scripture, such as Jesus' words "I am the resurrection and the life" and one or two simple prayers. I say, "Tell him how you feel. Let him bring you his comfort. Give him a chance to meet you in your need," and I go back the next day when they have had a chance to be alone.

There are many times when, as I leave bereaved people and get into my car, I weep for them, especially when they are friends, people I know, members of our church. It is impossible to be detached, to be unaffected. Jesus himself was affected deeply by the death of his friend and the grief of the bereaved sisters. Perhaps one of the most poignant verses in the Bible is the shortest verse of all, "Jesus wept" (KJV). In those two words we have the picture of his identification with human suffering. In those two words lies the answer to those who say, "Why doesn't God do something?" Here we have our assurance of God's concern, God's love.

The God who weeps was misunderstood then as now. Some saw love; others saw indifference. It is the same today as we look out on the suffering world and see across it the shadow of the cross. Some see in that cross the love of God, the self-giving God; for others it is the sign of failure and of defeat.

Death comes to us all. It can come at any time. Some fight it long and hard; others wait for it, indeed would welcome it. Often it is unexpected; a split second separates life from death. The great and famous have their death reported in the news, and splendid services are held. Those who meet their death through violence often have attending TV cameras, and the funeral may be the grounds for demonstration and further violence. But most deaths pass unnoticed, except by a few. The local paper carries a brief announcement; the shoppers barely glance at the hearse going slowly along the street on the way to the cemetery.

Death is inevitable. It is the one sure fact of life. From the moment we come into the world, we are on our way out of it. Death catches up with us all in the end. Death is the last word— or is it?

What of the one who says, "I am the resurrection and the life"? How can anyone claim to be that? Who does he think he is—God?

Chapter 3

Moment of truth

John 11:38-54

BLONDIN WAS THE most famous acrobat of all time; he per-
formed the seemingly impossible by crossing Niagara Falls on a
tightrope. The crowd held their breath as he did what had never been
done before—the most death-defying performance ever witnessed.

When he reached the other side, he asked the crowd whether
they believed he could do it again. Yes, they believed he could!
But what if he were blindfolded *and* pushed a wheelbarrow across
and twirled an umbrella at the same time? Oh yes, they believed he
could! And what if he carried a man on his back? Who believed he
could do that as well? Many expressed their confidence. Then he
asked for a volunteer—that was a different story!

How many who said they believed Blondin could perform the
feat would have taken up his challenge, even after seeing him cross
once? Many believed he could do it, but few would have put their
faith to the test. Would you? I often wonder who had to have the
greater faith: Blondin or the man on his back. I suppose the difference was that Blondin had faith in himself, while the man on
his back had to put his faith in Blondin; he was totally dependent
on Blondin to get him across and could do nothing but trust him.

As Jesus went to the grave of his friend Lazarus, what did
Martha and Mary and the people who were with them think he was
going to do? To pay his respects? To weep? Martha and Mary both
had affirmed their belief that Jesus could have prevented the death
of their brother *if* he had arrived in time. Martha had declared her
faith in Jesus as the Son of God, the one who could bring life out
of death. How did she feel as Jesus approached her brother's tomb?

Then Jesus spoke. "Take away the stone," he ordered. You can almost hear the intake of breath as he said those words. Silence descended; no one moved. Then Martha, in a down-to-earth statement, voiced what they were all thinking, what they all feared to experience. "Lord, already there is a stench because he has been dead four days." The King James Version of the Bible puts it even more strongly: "Lord, by this time he stinketh." Martha was right. Four days dead in a hot climate, the smell and the sight would be terrible indeed. Anyone who has lived in such a climate knows only too well that burial must follow death as quickly as possible for that reason. Decay sets in swiftly; the body must be removed immediately.

Jesus reminded Martha of what he had told her and what she had affirmed; there was no more protest. The stone was moved out of position, the seal was broken, and Jesus gave thanks to his Father in heaven for listening to him, thanking his Father that the people would see God's glory. In doing so, he testified to the power of God, staking his all on God's action. He gave a visual aid to the power of prayer, so the people might know that God answers prayer, that God is the giver of life, that God has power over death itself. Jesus raised his eyes to heaven. He thereby caused those who stood with him at the graveside to raise their eyes to heaven, to God. Jesus gave his Father all the glory.

Then came the word of command: "Lazarus, come out!" And out of the grave came no bad smell but the living man Lazarus. Imagine the sight—the man walking out of the grave, from death into life, covered with the clothing of the dead. It must have been an awesome sight. Some may have thought it was a ghost or a vision. The trappings of death were removed; they were not needed. Lazarus was alive and well. He had been brought not only back to life but back from the process of decay. He stood before them, the evidence and proof of the power of God, the testament to God's glory. There could be no argument. He had died. He had been buried. He should have been a stinking corpse. No way could anyone explain away this living man. The moment of truth had taken place there before their very eyes.

What more did anyone need to believe Jesus? What more could they ask? For many it was enough, but that did not mean that they all wanted to follow Jesus. Quite the opposite! A council meeting of religious leaders was called. Whether Jesus had really raised Lazarus was not disputed—how could it be? But the purpose of their meeting was not to rejoice with Lazarus or to give God the glory or to accept Jesus as the one whom God had sent to them. It was to decide how to get rid of Jesus. The religious leaders could not allow him to go around raising people from the dead—that was dangerous; it could mean trouble. They could put up with the preaching, tolerate some of his healings (those could always be explained away if they worked hard enough at it), but raising people from the dead was too much. Jesus would have to go. He was a troublemaker, a danger to the lives, comfort, and status of the religious leaders.

Jesus is still a danger and for the same reason. He brings the dead to life. For that reason, Christians, those who follow Jesus, are seen as dangerous even today in many parts of the world. Councils pronounce sentence on them. They are too dangerous to be allowed to live.

If Jesus had been just a teacher, one who taught a way of life that was part of a moral, caring, serving system; if he had just preached a gospel of love and peace, then he could have been accepted quite happily. It would have been acceptable to have had a few people healed—after all, these things do happen from time to time, for various reasons. Even the medical profession acknowledges that sometimes symptoms disappear on their own, illnesses clear up, and there is the mystery of long-term remission. If people have faith that something is helping, then maybe it can. We have all heard of the colored water that seems to do the trick because it is believed to be medicine. It's all in the mind; there is a perfectly logical explanation.

A teaching, preaching, even healing Jesus can be tolerated in any society. He can take his place alongside all the other so-called "gods" to be nodded at now and again and used to grace ceremonial occasions—he cannot do any harm, and there is always a possibility that he may do a little good, if you like that sort of thing. If, however, he is the Son of God, if he has brought others to life, if he is alive and active in the world, then he is dangerous. He cannot be allowed to go free, and neither can those who claim to belong to him, who say they have authority to continue his work in his way and in his power.

What sort of Jesus do we believe in, I wonder. Do we believe he has raised the dead to life? Did he actually bring to life a man who had been dead for four days, or is it just a story, an illustration of a spiritual truth, or even perhaps a gross exaggeration? Raising the dead to life is hard to accept for sophisticated men and women in our technological age, when even some leaders in his church explain away such events, write learned books on the subject, and tell us that "in the light of experience," it could not have happened and therefore did not happen.

Perhaps the majority of those who watched Blondin cross the gap between earth and sky believed he could do it again; they would raise their hands and give him their vote of confidence. They had faith in him, but the test of their faith was whether they were personally willing to be carried by him across the gap. Jesus was the one person who, in modern language, had the faith to "put his money where his mouth was" and risk everything, even life itself. In return he shared the triumph and the glory.

It reminds me of the saying "If he is not Lord of all, he is not Lord at all." Faith means staking everything on Jesus Christ, allowing him to carry us across the gap—and with no safety net either!

Did he raise the dead, or didn't he? Could he? Can he? Will he? Dare we risk the stone being rolled away from the tomb that holds our own fears, our own death and decay? What if all that comes out is a bad smell?... But then that is the risk we must take if we really want to know.

Chapter 4

Home for the feast

John 11:55-57

To GO HOME for Christmas is the hope of most people, whatever their age. They may have spread their wings and gone
off to distant places to live and work; they may have families of
their own and have settled into a new community; but as Christmastime approaches, all thoughts go to "home." Where their parents live, where the family home is, there they belong.

When Christmas week arrives, our airports, railway stations, and
bus depots are crowded with folks, heavily laden with suitcases
and packages, "going home." Traveling at Christmastime is quite
different from normal travel. People talk to each other; they smile,
exchange confidences; some even sing on the way! For those not
able to get home, messages via mail, telephone, or e-mail span the
miles, as the next best thing to being with loved ones at the fes-
tive season.

At the other end, preparations are being made to receive the
family members coming home: rooms are prepared; favorite dishes
cooked; the decorations and trees with shining lights say, "Welcome home!" Then comes the joy of reunion as the plane touches
down, the train pulls in, buses arrive, the car turns into the drive-
way. There are hugs and kisses, laughter and tears; the family is
complete; they are all home for Christmas.

The Feast of the Passover in Jesus' time wasn't quite like our
Christmas. It was far more a religious obligation than a family celebration, but the two holidays have much in common. Everyone
wanted to be home for Passover, and "home" for every Jew was—
and still is—Jerusalem. It was obligatory for all male Jews who lived

within fifteen miles of Jerusalem to get there, regardless of the inconvenience, but they would come from much farther afield. The journey was seen not just as a duty but as a joy.

The road to Jerusalem would be a continuous stream of people. No planes, coaches, or cars—they walked! And so the roads were put into good order, the bridges repaired, ready for the pilgrims who were on their way home for the feast from far and wide. For the pilgrims themselves, there would be eager exchanges of news, plenty of gossip and speculation, and there would be the singing of psalms, rejoicing in God and his greatness, psalms of deliverance, psalms of victory.

One big problem overshadowed all else, though. The Jewish people were under an army of occupation. They may have been in their own homeland, but they were subject to their occupying power, Rome. The people resented and hated the fact that, although they had been delivered by God out of Egypt all those years ago, they were now once more in captivity. In their longing to be free, they looked for a deliverer, a savior. And at Passover time especially, nationalistic feelings ran high, fanning the flames of bitterness and resentment, so that the crowds of pilgrims on their way to Jerusalem were not exactly happy, carefree travelers. Excited, yes. Full of purpose and idealism, yes. Delighted to be with their fellows, yes. But, oh that circumstances were different! They longed to be free as they advanced upon their beloved Jerusalem.

For the Romans, Passover time was one big headache, a time to be on "full alert." It was never easy, being the occupying army. There was no love lost between the Jews and the Romans. The rule of the sword, the fear of the lash, the shadow of the cross kept the Jews in submission, but the Romans knew that at any time there could be an uprising of these fanatically nationalistic people. The only authority the Jews took notice of was their religious leaders, so the Romans knew it was prudent to cultivate these, giving them some concessions in return for using their influence to keep the more passionate nationalists under control.

This Passover there was another complication—Jesus of Nazareth. Many rumors were flying around about him. He had achieved a large following, mostly among the ordinary folk, with his teaching and preaching and reported healings. He had become rather too popular. Some were even saying he was the Savior, the promised deliverer sent from God. If reports were to be believed, he had even raised a man from the dead! So he could prove very dangerous indeed. He had not been greeted favorably or with acclaim by the religious leaders of his people. Oh yes, there were some who were important who secretly agreed with him—but he was too "way out." He didn't conform to the accepted patterns. He could cause real trouble for those who had settled into an uneasy truce with the Romans, those who chose peace at any price.

The Romans did not want any more trouble. They had enough on their hands already, with so many people on the move for Passover, and there was always the danger of riots and confrontation. They hoped the Jewish authorities would sort this Jesus out among themselves. It would be easier and cleaner if they did. If it was a religious argument, then let the religious leaders deal with it. All the Romans wanted was for Passover to pass over as quietly and as peaceably as possible, then to get back to normal routine.

The chief priests and Pharisees didn't want Jesus around at the Passover, for there was always the possibility that the crowds might find in him what they were looking for. They might get ideas about making him a king or a ruler, ousting the present religious authorities. Orders were given that anyone who knew where Jesus was should disclose it, so that he might be "attended to" and taken into custody before he could influence any more people.

Jesus, quite aware of their plans, quietly went with friends to Ephraim, north of Jerusalem, "out in the sticks." There he was safe, away from the mainstream, away from those who for various reasons wanted to dispose of him.

For the pilgrims going up to Jerusalem, Jesus was the main topic of conversation. Many had stories to tell of hearing and seeing him. He was the focus of speculation. The crowds were not stupid; they knew what was going on, the plans that were being made to get rid of him. They knew, too, that he was a most extraordinary person. It was impossible to be neutral about him. He demanded a response. So, on the road to Jerusalem, views for and against were fiercely expressed, and the big question was, "Surely [Jesus] will not come to the festival, will he?" Some may have said, "If he knows what's good for him, he will keep away. He would be a fool to come; he would walk straight into trouble." Yet others, knowing that Jesus was a religious Jew, who always observed the festivals, felt sure that he would come. He would perform his obligation, whether it meant his arrest or not. There were those who had hoped that if and when he came, his arrival would launch the big showdown between the Jews and the Romans: Jesus would lead them to victory; God would enable him to destroy the occupying powers; this Passover could be a time of rejoicing and triumph.

Just a few days to go! Excitement was at fever pitch; Jerusalem was getting even more crowded; people were on the move; everything was coming to a head. And Jesus, where was he now? He too was on the move, to visit friends, to enjoy a meal with some very special friends indeed—Mary, Martha, and the one who came back from the dead, Lazarus, their brother. It was to be a party with a difference, in more ways than one; for, though his friends did not know it, this visit would be the last opportunity Jesus would have to be with them, the last opportunity for them to show him how much they loved him. And what happened was recorded for all time, for us too to ponder over, to consider our verdict on love's extravagance.

Chapter 5

A celebration dinner

John 12:1-11

SITTING OVER LUNCH in the canteen after a hard morning's
work of recording programs when I was the Anglican Religious
Adviser at Yorkshire Television, two of us were chatting about all
sorts of subjects, including the weather and the government. Then
suddenly out of the blue my companion said, "If Lazarus came back
from the dead, why aren't we told what he said when he came
back? He surely must have said something!"

I must admit the question threw me, because it's true that we
have a record of the raising of Lazarus, and he is mentioned several times, but we hear nothing from his own mouth. We have a
very full description of the scene, of the conversation between the
sisters, Martha and Mary, and Jesus, but from Lazarus—nothing.

My immediate answer was that the Gospels don't record everything that happened in the ministry of Jesus or every conversation.
The Gospels offer a condensed picture. But what we have gives us
sufficient information to grasp who Jesus was and how he lived
here on earth. We have the outstanding situations; examples of his
attitudes toward all sorts of people; the highlights of his teaching,
preaching, and healing ministry. The Gospels are rather like a family photograph album, with a series of snapshots, rather than a
diary. I quoted to my friend some words from near the end of John's
Gospel: "Now Jesus did many other signs in the presence of his
disciples, which are not written in this book. But these are written
so that you may come to believe that Jesus is the Messiah, the Son
of God, and that through believing you may have life in his name"
(John 20:30-31).

My questioner, although obviously impressed with my ability to quote chapter and verse, was still not satisfied. He protested, "But it would help people like me to believe if we could read the account of dying and coming back by the person it happened to."

I can understand my questioner. It would have been helpful to have been able to read the actual words Lazarus spoke. But it is quite clear that he did die, that he came back from the dead, and was still around some time later, alive and well and enjoying a meal at home with his family. In fact, his sisters, Martha and Mary, prepared a special celebration dinner for their friends, and Jesus was the guest of honor at it. Martha, true to form, helped to serve the meal. We can imagine her busy, fussing, happy to do what she loved doing, giving pleasure to family and friends by putting on a good spread. It was her way of saying thank you to Jesus, showing her love for him in a practical way.

There is a retreat house in Yorkshire, run by the Sisters of the Order of the Holy Paraclete. It is just a couple of miles away from Whitby, tucked away from the main road amid the most glorious countryside. When I was there on retreat, one of the things that impressed me was the obvious joy the sisters found in serving their guests—the pleasure on their faces as they dished up the meals or poured out the coffee. I can see now one of the sisters cleaning the windows with an expression of blissful happiness. I saw this joy in the way they all worked together, in the extra little touches such as flowers in the bedrooms, how the meals were arranged, and the shine on the furniture. That service was, for them, part of their joyful commitment to God; nothing was too much because it was a labor of love. I owe a lot to the loving Marthas of the Order of the Holy Paraclete at Sleights!

I think too of those in our parish who delight to serve in the very mundane, practical things like cleaning the church, repairing the woodwork, tidying the surrounding gardens, keeping the linen in good repair—all labors of love. If I asked those people to get up and preach a sermon, to teach in Sunday school, or even to read a lesson, they would run a mile, and yet they equally serve their Lord in the generous and unstinting way they give of themselves in the down-to-earth practical things. We thank God for all the Marthas!

And what about Mary? We read that "they" prepared a dinner. I like to think that Mary had done her fair share in the preparation but then let her sister bask in the glory of being the hostess—not to get out of helping to serve but to let her sister have the honor of being in charge of the celebrations. The food was the very best they could provide; nothing was too good for the Master, the one who had given them back their brother from the dead, the one who they knew would give them all eternal life beyond the grave.

Mary, full of love, also gave of her best to Jesus. She gave the most precious thing she possessed, an expensive perfume which represented her life's savings. She didn't hand it to him; she humbly poured it over his feet, and then, as an act of loving abandonment, wiped his feet with her hair.

What did the guests think of her action? I imagine some would have been embarrassed at such an emotional exhibition; others puzzled, surprised, impressed by the magnitude of the gift and the expression of it. When I read the account I can almost smell that perfume. John says, "The house was filled with the fragrance of the perfume," and that sweet smell of love's extravagance fills the room where I, two thousand years later, recall that moment. It is one of the most beautiful acts of love ever recorded in history. It is the supreme example of a loving heart's response.

Yet when it happened, one man was very annoyed indeed. He could see only the monetary value of the perfume. To him it was sheer waste. He did not see or smell love; the act left a sour taste in his mouth. He was angry with the giver—she must be mad! What a waste! If she had wanted to give away the perfume, why hadn't she sold it so that the money could have been used to give practical help to poor people?

He had a point, hadn't he? After all, he was the one who looked after the cash side of things, the one who had to pay the bills. He had been entrusted by Jesus and the others to take charge of the finances. He could have done so much more with that perfume—or with the realized value of it—and now it was wasted! All that was left was the smell, and soon that would evaporate.

How wrong he was! That sweet smell of love has never evaporated. It has filled the whole world and has prompted others to give their all in thanksgiving for what Jesus has done for them in their lives.

The Gospel account tells us that the man who objected was the one who soon would betray Jesus for just one-tenth of the value of that perfume—Judas Iscariot. We are told he was a thief, who betrayed the confidence that had been put in him. I still wonder, though, whether he actually stole the money for himself, or whether it was just that he saw everything in cash terms, since he was the elected treasurer. It may be that he saw the kingdom of God only in terms of an earthly kingdom, which inevitably would need cash support. He may have been a very efficient steward of the group's resources. I don't know, I can't judge. All I can do is feel very sorry for him. He missed out on the joy because he was only bothered about the tinkle of coins. He could not smell the sweetness because of his own acidity of life.

There are still those today who see the kingdom of God in terms of money. Their commitment to Christ is in relation to the smallest coin in their pocket. I have been in churches when we have all sung the hymn "Take my life, and let it be consecrated, Lord, to thee" with great vigor, and the words "Take my silver and my gold; not a mite would I withhold" with rousing enthusiasm—and then I have received the offertory plate and seen only small change! It has been said that the last part of a person to be converted is the pocket. Books are written, sermons preached, campaigns arranged, all to encourage the faithful to give to the Lord, and very few respond with more than a token amount.

It is not only our money with which we are mean, of course. How stinting we are in offering ourselves, our time, our abilities, our love! Most of us measure out these offerings carefully rather than pour them out generously. Why did Mary give her all, and so emotionally? Wasn't it because she knew and appreciated what Jesus had done for her?

Mary did what she knew she had to do when she poured out her fragrant offering over the feet of her Lord—she responded to the opportunity she had to show her love. That special moment would never come again; she took it when it came, oblivious to what others thought of her action. How many times are we prompted within to do some act of kindness, take a certain course of action, make a generous gesture—and then have second thoughts? What will others think of us? Is it the most sensible thing to do? Wouldn't it be better to wait until later? So we hesitate, and we are lost because the time has gone; we had our opportunity and we did not rise to it.

I remember some words written in my autograph book many years ago: "I expect to pass through this world but once; any good thing therefore that I can do or any kindness that I can show to any fellow creature, let me do it now; let me not defer or neglect it, for I shall not pass this way again."

So we have Martha, whose joy it was to serve, and Mary, whose delight it was to give. And what of Lazarus? He was the living witness at the celebration. He spoke by his very presence. The people gathered to see Jesus, who had raised a man from the dead, and Lazarus, who was that man. Here was the evidence people looked for, the evidence that tipped the scales in favor of Jesus. And yet, while many people rejoiced, others were plotting to wipe out the evidence. Lazarus, too, must be destroyed; for while he lived, that man who came back from the dead would attract men and women to follow Jesus.

When we become Christians, we come out of death into life. We are the living witnesses, to be seen in our homes, at work, in the community, as well as in our church activities. Do those who meet us know we are different? What effect do we have on them? If we are true witnesses, then we will have the same effect as Lazarus. We will be the living proof of Jesus Christ, and some will come to believe in him, but others will hate us, and they will seek to remove us. As Christians we have to be willing to accept the consequences for his sake, whatever that may mean.

Chapter 6

The victory parade
John 12:12-22

I GREW UP IN a small Cheshire town. We lived a couple of miles from the town center, and I remember that as a child it was quite an adventure to go "down into town." It was a very ordinary sort of place with not a great deal of excitement, so when there was a special event, everybody turned out for it. One of the events I remember vividly was the homecoming of a local soldier who had won a medal for valor, the Victoria Cross, during the war.

He was a very ordinary fellow by all accounts. Some people shook their heads and said he was a bit of a cutup; others said that going into the army had been the making of him. Anyway, he had shown great bravery, was awarded the Victoria Cross (VC), and had been promoted to sergeant, so it was decided to have a "Welcome Home" for him in the town. I stood with my friends and enthusiastically waved my flag, and everybody cheered. The cheering got louder and louder, and folk were jumping up and down. Then came the sound of the band, and we could see some of the local dignitaries standing up on a truck and with them the smiling, khaki-clad figure of our war hero. I can recall him now; he looked so big and handsome with his sergeant's stripes on his arms and the shining medal on his chest for all to see. We all got hoarse from shouting and cheering. It was a marvelous day.

Some years later I saw the war hero in the town. In ordinary clothes and without all the trappings of uniform and medal, he looked very insignificant, much smaller than he had seemed standing on the truck. Looking back, I suppose it was all the excitement of the day—the cheering, the bunting, the being part of an exuberant crowd—that had made the event so thrilling. I had been carried along with the crowd, caught up in the magic of it all.

Whenever I read the account of Jesus' coming into Jerusalem on the first Palm Sunday, I remember that victory parade in Congleton, Cheshire, with all of us waiting for the hero to come and making sure he got a glorious reception. Jesus came into Jerusalem as a hero too—after all, he had fed the hungry, healed the sick, raised the dead; there was nothing he could not do. The ordinary people, who had been downtrodden for so long under Roman oppression, who looked for the king, the messiah promised by God, at last had real hope. They could see their king. He was here at last. For them it was not only a political occasion but a spiritual one, for the messiah was God's anointed. Nothing, and no one, would be able to stand against him, and the people would share in his victory. No wonder they cheered. No wonder they waved the palms. No wonder they shouted, "Hosanna!" "Praise God!"

And Jesus the King came—on a donkey. It really was ridiculous, a king on a donkey! So why a donkey? Those people who understood the scriptures would know that it was not by accident but in direct fulfillment of the words of the prophet Zechariah:

> Rejoice greatly, O daughter Zion!
> Shout aloud, O daughter Jerusalem!
> Lo, your king comes to you;
> triumphant and victorious is he,
> humble and riding on a donkey,
> on a colt, the foal of a donkey. (Zech. 9:9)

Maybe some in the crowd remembered this prophecy and knew that this was the promised one who would deliver them, but even they would fail to grasp what sort of a victory it was to be. Later on they would shake their heads sadly and say, "We had hoped that he was the one to redeem Israel" (Luke 24:21). Gradually for some, dramatically for others, the truth would sink in. They would realize that the king did indeed enter Jerusalem on that day, and that his kingdom has no end.

On the day, though, all the crowd could think was, *Freedom at last! Victory is ours. Jesus is king. Life from now on will be altogether different.* They thought they would be free forever.

Yes, they were right! Jesus would free them from sin, from death, for he was the one who raised people from the dead. He was the giver of life but not quite as they had imagined. His new lifestyle was not the gift of an earthly king to his loyal subjects but the gift of eternal life for all who would trust him as Savior and as Lord.

The cheers went on and on, and the crowd got bigger and more excited, and the praise and adulation rang stronger. The Pharisees were in deep trouble. They sensed they were in danger of defeat; they were losing out to Jesus. He was the hero of the day. "Look, the world has gone after him!" they commented bitterly, and they were right. Jesus had captured the hearts of all in the city. Even the foreigners were following him. The world had gathered in Jerusalem. The world had glimpsed the glory of God in the man on the donkey.

The Pharisees were powerless—for a time. Soon, though, they would gather their forces and throw everything into destroying Jesus. They would even seem to succeed. They would nail him down—that would silence the crowd; after all, what use is a dead hero?

Two thousand years have gone by since the King rode in on a donkey. He is still riding in, humbly yet regally, into men's and women's hearts and lives. The world still goes after him, and nothing can stop him.

The world came to Jerusalem. Many came to worship—not only Jews but those who were seekers after God, who wanted to know and understand the things of God—the religious, the curious, the pious, and the puzzled.

There were also those who came along to see the show, to "watch the world go by." Among them were some Greeks, who were there for the festival. Jesus interested them, and they wanted to meet him, so they approached Philip. Why Philip? Maybe his Greek name gave them the confidence to approach him—or his friendly nature. He could have been pointed out as someone who would introduce them to Jesus, or then again it might have been that Philip saw they were wanting help and offered it. Who knows? Anyway, Philip told Andrew, and together they approached Jesus, for they knew he would turn no one away.

And so it is still. But whoever does come to Jesus will be left with no false illusions as to what following him means. It means handing over everything. It is total commitment, even to death. It means risking all you have, and in exchange—life and glory! The terms and conditions of service are plainly laid out. Jesus makes sure that those who wish to follow him know the cost—and the reward. Whether they take up his offer or not is entirely up to each individual.

Many today say wistfully, "We would like to see Jesus." They are outsiders, standing on the edge and watching what is going on in the Christian church. They see the trappings of faith. They hear the arguments, read the reports, witness the ceremonies. Something within them stirs, questions, responds, but they need to be able to get to the heart of what it's all about. They need to see Jesus for themselves.

I talk to all sorts of people, and I find that many who do not claim to be Christians, and who never come to church, are still fascinated with Jesus. They want to know more, but who can they ask? Who dare they approach? I discover that many have tried to inquire but have met with a blank wall. Some have ventured into churches and have not been welcomed, so have not tried again. Sadly I have to admit that this is often true. We have our cozy church "clubs," our own circle of Christian friends who are like ourselves, with whom we feel comfortable. We do not take kindly to outsiders—especially if they are different, if they don't speak our language or don't know the rules.

The glory of Jesus is that he is for the world—for everyone. It was so hard for people to understand that when he was here on earth. His friends wanted to keep him for their exclusive use—

after all, he was a Jew; he had come to fulfill the law and the prophets (Matt. 5:17); he was "king of the Jews" (Matt. 2:2). One of the biggest problems of the church after Pentecost was to realize that Gentiles did not have to become Jews before they could be accepted by Jesus; they were accepted as themselves. And what about the position of women? Jesus afforded to women the same privileges as men; they could be his friends; they were equally valued and loved. But even today the church struggles with the position of women, often relegating them to the menial tasks of church life, refusing them the joy of serving their Lord as ministers, pastors, or teachers.

It was to the Pharisee Nicodemus that Jesus spoke the words of invitation, available for all (the story is in chapter 3 of John's Gospel): "So must the Son of Man be lifted up, that whoever believes in him may have eternal life. For God so loved the world that he gave his only Son, so that everyone who believes in him may not perish but may have eternal life" (3:14-16). That promise was for the Pharisees and for the dying thief crucified with Jesus, for the Roman soldiers who hammered in the nails, for the persecutor of Christians, Saul, later called Paul. It was for the small known world of yesterday and for the citizens of today's "global village"—for all races, colors, cultures. For the gifted undergraduate, the child who will never progress beyond the mental age of a baby, the privileged owner of the stately home, and the one who resides in prison.

When Jesus saw the Greeks coming to meet him, he knew that the glory of God was being revealed, that the time was almost at hand when he would be literally "lifted up" before the whole world. That glory meant death on the cross, before the glory of heaven.

So what difference does it make to me? I know all this. I know that Jesus died for the world—for the good, the bad, and the very indifferent. Yet I have to ask myself: Do I share him with the world, my world? What have I got to say to the person who wastes my time, makes impossible demands upon me, uses me? Do I show that person the glory of the Lord, or am I hiding it? Whom do I include in my world? I must confess that my world is mainly the people I choose to be part of it. What conceit! It is not my world at all; it is God's world. I am part of God's world. I am loved and wanted and so are all the rest.

Although I may not like it, I am forced to accept the value of every other person, whoever and whatever he or she is—and Jesus wants that person to meet him and to get to know him. So what am I to answer when the request comes, "We would like to see Jesus"? Is there anything in me that will prompt that request? I wonder. I do indeed wonder.

Chapter 7

Which way to glory?

John 12:23-50

No pain, no palm; no thorns, no throne;
no gall, no glory; no cross, no crown.

THE WORDS ARE by William Penn (1644–1718), the English Quaker who founded the American colony of Pennsylvania. In his stark alternatives we see the choice that faces all of us. If only there were a way around, a detour we could take to avoid the pain, the thorns, the gall, and the cross! If only we could slip off the road and rejoin it later, having avoided the uneven surface and the pitted track, so that we would just have to coast down the final straight! If God is God, we tell ourselves, if God loves and cares for us, if God rules supreme over earth and heaven, then surely God would point out a detour to us, wave us through, and meet us at the other end, having cleared all obstacles away and given us an easy passage.

Jesus must have had feelings like these. He did not look forward to suffering, to having his life ended so horribly and brutally. He did not like the look of the journey ahead. He was still a young man, at the height of his strength and powers. Life apparently lay ahead, full of endless possibilities. He had just begun to make real headway; at last his message was beginning to get through, not only to his friends and his own people but also to the world. The horizon was widening; the sky was the limit. He prayed that glory might be brought to his Father's name, and God spoke those words of assurance: "I have glorified it, and I will glorify it again."

Over and over again, Jesus had brought glory to God: in his birth, in his baptism, through his ministry. But there was no short cut to the final glory. Jesus knew he would be lifted up before all the world, present and to come, but at what cost to himself! The voice of God assured him of the glory; but more than that, God assured the world that what was to come was the culmination of a glorious plan for all humanity. The approaching event was not a horrible disaster or mistake but the way of final triumph.

The crowd heard something but did not recognize the voice of God. They knew something had happened. Some explained it away naturally—"it was thunder." Others felt it was more than a coincidence; it was an angel talking to Jesus but not to them. They did not hear the voice of divine approval. If they had heard, then maybe they would have taken notice of the one who stood before them.

If the crowd had known what a short a time Jesus would be with them, maybe they would have listened to him. Maybe they would have let go of their own ideas and been willing to let him shed light on what confused them, what they didn't understand, and what didn't seem to make sense. Jesus made one last appeal to them, offering them the light they needed. They had seen him give sight to the blind. He had proved he was a giver of the light. He had stood before them and declared, "I have come as light into the world" (v. 46). He had offered them the light of life, but for the most part they didn't want to see or know.

What more could he do? He had offered them everything, proved his words by his deeds, and still they did not believe in him. It seemed impossible, and yet it was true. So Jesus left them and went away. John records the words of the prophet Isaiah:

> "Lord, who has believed our message,
>   and to whom has the arm of the Lord been revealed?"
> And so they could not believe, because Isaiah also said,
>   "He has blinded their eyes and hardened their heart,

so that they might not look with their eyes,
and understand with their heart and turn—
and I would heal them" (vv. 38-40).

Isaiah had prophesied that when the messiah came, he would not
be accepted. People would be blind to him because they were so
sure they knew what God would do and how God would act. They
had become hardened, and so they were unable to see God at work
right there in their midst. It was tragic when you think about it.
Jesus was with them, right there—they saw him, witnessed him at
work, heard his words—and yet they did not see, did not want to
see. It seems beyond belief.

Beyond belief! Is he beyond belief today, even though we can
see him at work and hear his words? Or are we still too tied up in
arguments, blindly yet cleverly using words of scripture for our
own purposes? "You can make the Bible prove anything you want
it to"—how often I have heard that! Shame on us, that we take the
Word of God and use it to suit ourselves. We pick and choose, dis-
miss the parts we do not like or understand, and finish up with a
pretty package that fits neatly and safely into the space we have allo-
cated to it. There it stays, just another of the "coffee table books"—
to dress up our living room rather than address our lives. Perhaps
we know in our heart of hearts that if we did accept the whole,
including the parts we do not like or understand, it would mean a
new way of life, and that would be dangerous!

Some of the Jewish authorities knew that what Jesus said was
true. The light did break upon them, but they turned away because
their own way of life without Jesus was more comfortable than life
with him. They did not want any trouble, so they kept quiet. They
knew the truth all right, but that was as far as it went. What other
people thought of them mattered more than God. "They loved
human glory more than the glory that comes from God." What
sad words. What a condemnation!

Something I find fascinating when I visit a new place is reading old epitaphs in the churches and churchyards. They provide

a valuable insight not only into the lives of particular individuals but into the society of their time. Some read like character references, the life of the departed being described in such glowing terms. Like references, they often required reading between the lines! The ones that really say something positive are not the glowing accounts of the departed's achievements but those with just a simple cross or a word of scripture that bears a challenge to the living.

Perhaps none of us will have any say as to what is carved on our headstone; it will be left to those who have to see to such arrangements, unless of course we have left instructions in our will! Whether what is written is the opinion of our friends or the instructions we leave behind doesn't really matter. What matters is the approval or disapproval of God. God will not write it on our tombstone. God will face us with it when we meet.

Will you have the approval of God when you stand before God? Will I? I know this: as I look at my life, I do not have the confidence to hold it before God and say, "Look what I have done, what I have achieved, what others have said about me!" But I take heart and confidence from what Jesus promised. I will be accepted by God because I have put my faith and trust in Jesus, "who loved me and gave himself for me" (Gal. 2:20). In the words of Charles Wesley,

> No condemnation now I dread;
> Jesus, and all in him, is mine;
> alive in him, my living Head,
> and clothed in righteousness divine,
> bold I approach th' eternal throne,
> and claim the crown, through Christ my own.

The authority I have for this is Jesus! His promise to me. His promise offered and accepted.

Jesus offers life. He has been offering it for two thousand years. Always there are those who refuse his offer, who do not believe him, in spite of the evidence. Then there are those who believe him but consider other things of more importance—like status, a quiet life, money in the bank, an absorbing hobby, the demands of the family, the pressure of the job, the power of high office . . . . But then, we have the choice. It all depends on what we really want—in the end.

Chapter 8 ⟶

Be my guest
John 13:1-20

IT HAS BEEN the inspiration for artists, musicians, and writers. It is seen as a symbol of love and unity; and also of division and rejection. The wise and learned seek to explain it; the humble accept it with awe and wonder. It is reenacted wherever the name of Jesus Christ is known, and, as you read this, men and women in many different places and circumstances will be taking part in the portrayal of what happened two thousand years ago in an upper room in Jerusalem.

For Christians, what happened in that room was the embodiment of God's purpose for humankind, made known in Jesus Christ. Each person looks at the event and makes it what each desires. Many Christians have taken the mystery of that occasion and translated it, sought to confine it to the level of human understanding. To emphasize its importance, it has been clothed with the magnificence of earthly power, embellished with the jewels of earth, expanded with human eloquence. It has been given glowing descriptive titles, like neon signs lighting up a theater, "rave reviews" shouting to command attention, inviting us in to the performance. But sometimes it is so grand, so exclusive, so expensive that although we long to share in it, we are not deemed fit to enter the reenactment; we are disqualified by being what we are; we could not cope with the regulations stipulated even if we would enter and be part of it. Those "in the know," those who belong, guard the door. They only allow us to watch the comings and goings of the participants, to get a glimpse as the door is opened for them, but that is all.

What did happen at that special meal we call the Last Supper? We will not find the answer to our question by looking at forms and ceremonies, even by looking at artists' impressions or listening to glorious choral offerings. We can find out for ourselves only by going back to the beginning, by going into that upstairs room, taking our place at the table, accepting the host's invitation to the supper.

Some time ago my husband, Peter, and I were guests at a very special celebration. A couple of hundred people sat down to a most delightful meal, and as it was fairly informal there was no seating plan; we just sat where we wanted. There were enough places for all the invited guests, and we found ourselves with some people whom we knew well, some whom we knew slightly, and most of whom we knew not at all. What we had in common was that we had all been invited by the host. We were his guests; he and what he was, our meeting point. Chatting with other guests over the meal was quite fascinating as we discovered quite a bit about one another. By the end of the evening we had opened up to each other in quite a deep way. If it had not been for our host, I don't suppose I would ever have talked to some of those people. We were poles apart, yet it was surprising, once we did open up, just how much we had in common.

A week or so later, I met with a group of colleagues at a conference where we were reenacting the Last Supper. We had to decide which disciple we felt was most like ourselves and take his place. In fact, we discovered, the disciples really fell into three types—the conformists, the revolutionaries, and the reconcilers. And so we divided ourselves into those three groupings and made our group contribution to that dramatic portrayal of the Last Supper. It was an enlightening exercise. There were real surprises as to where people saw themselves, and the exercise revealed tensions within our conferences. Sparks began to fly, hurts were expressed, sides were taken. But the marvelous thing was that when we joined in sharing the bread and wine, as we both received from and gave to one another, we discovered concern and love for one another because we realized we were all guests at the table of the Lord.

The friends of Jesus were in the upper room by invitation; they were there purely because of Jesus. Each one wanted to be with him, to share in that most intimate experience of friendship, eating together. They put up with the fellow guests because they had to! No doubt there were those who felt that the presence of some of the others spoiled their enjoyment—a pity they had been invited; it would have been much better without them! All of them wanted to be the Number One guest, to sit in the place of honor, and to be accorded the service they required.

Perhaps it sounds rather strong to say that of all of them, yet it must have been so, for not one of them was willing to perform the service of attending the needs of the others, that very basic need of a wash. They all sat there with the dirt of the streets on their feet, no doubt all tired, hot, unfit to sit down to a meal but all unwilling to make the move to serve. All were so concerned with themselves, with their position, that they denied themselves as well as the others the relief they needed. As a modern expression would put it, "they cut off their noses to spite their faces."

One of the guests, Judas, was no doubt preoccupied, lost in his own thoughts. He knew that soon he would be up and away on the traitor's path, away from Jesus, away from the circle of friends. Soon he would be slapped on the back for his betrayal; he would hold the bag of silver coins, his reward for delivering the goods, and with a kiss he would mark for death the one who offered life. Why should he do it? Surely after all the time with Jesus, he knew the reality of love, had learned from personal experience that Jesus alone had the answer for humankind? Could it have been that Judas was impatient with Jesus? Perhaps he thought to spur him on by his action, by putting him into the position of publicly and finally convincing his enemies of who he was. Did Judas really see himself as a double agent? We do not know the reason behind his betrayal, whether it was greed for himself or desire for the glory of the Lord. But Jesus knew, and whatever Judas was, Jesus loved him.

Jesus loved all his friends. The fact that soon he would be betrayed, denied, and deserted made no difference. He loved them, and all he saw as he looked at them was their need of someone to come along with a basin of cool water, to wash the dirt and grime of the road from them, to ease their hot and tired feet, so that they could relax and enjoy their meal without distraction. Without words or fuss, Jesus got up, fetched a basin, water, and a towel, and did what needed doing. He met their need. A very ordinary situation—hot and dirty feet needed washing, and Jesus did what was necessary.

I suppose most of us respond to the dramatic but not so easily to the mundane, yet equally needed, acts of kindness and consideration. A big disaster, a multiple pileup, a fire destroys blocks of houses, and help pours in. We see on TV the horror of famine and drought, and we reach for our checkbooks. The blond, blue-eyed child smiles at us from the screen, and we are quick to send a donation to pay for special medical attention. But what about the old lady who lives alone up the road? She is a bit odd, and the house— it does smell, and she wouldn't thank you for calling. And so you— and I—we don't. That young mother we see pushing a stroller in the mall—no one seems to bother with her. She looks as though she has been in a fight with someone (she had a black eye the other week); we have heard the man who lives with her beats her up; and he is a bit rough with the kids. But then what are the social services for? If we start interfering and asking questions, we might find ourselves drawn into a situation that has nothing to do with us. No, leave it to those whose job it is to care. Anyway she won't starve. No one does in this country, not like those abroad who don't have social security or medical insurance.

There is not much glamour or excitement in visiting "smelly" old people, nor in inviting a young mother and her runny-nosed baby into your home for tea. After all you don't want to get involved with other people's lives, and babies make such a mess! But then there wasn't much glamour or excitement in washing a dozen pairs of hot, sticky feet, was there? But Jesus did it. And he had this to say: "For I have set you an example, that you also should do as I have done to you." Somehow that sounds rather like a command,

and it seems to be directed at those who sit down at the Lord's table, who receive his loving offering, who have accepted his invitation to "be my guest," and who enjoy his company. It could be that he is saying it to you, and to me, if we count ourselves to be guests at his table. Couldn't it?

Chapter 9 ⟶

Could it be . . . me?

John 13:21-38

THE WORDS CAME as a bombshell: "One of you will betray me."

The friends looked at one another, stunned by the awful implications of what Jesus had just said. Of course, all of them knew that Jesus was in constant danger from those who opposed him—those who were jealous and afraid of him, who saw him as a threat to either their political or religious life. At any moment there might be a knock on the door, the command "Open up!" and Jesus could be arrested and taken from them by sheer brute force of men from outside. But to say that the enemy was within—one of them! Surely that was unthinkable, impossible!

How could anybody who had responded to the call of Jesus to be one of his special group of friends do such a thing? They had had three years of living together as a family of friends, three years of observing day in, day out the life of their Master, his public ministry, his private life, his relationship with God. Each one of them knew Jesus' love and care for them individually, having learned it firsthand from him, discovering what it meant to be part of the kingdom of God. How could any of them betray the one they followed, respected, and loved? Who could it possibly be?

Peter looked across to John sitting next to Jesus. Perhaps Jesus would tell John if he asked, so Peter motioned to John to ask him. Jesus did not name the betrayer but gave a clue: "It is the one to whom I give this piece of bread when I have dipped it in the dish." But none of them grasped what Jesus was talking about. It never occurred to them that it was Judas.

In two of the other Gospel accounts, those of Matthew (26:22) and Mark (14:19), the question is put rather differently. The friends ask Jesus, "Surely not I, Lord?"

Yes, they were jittery and anxious. Perhaps some of them thought back to times when they had questioned Jesus, when maybe twinges of doubt had crept into their minds, or they had been tempted to give up and go back home. It had not been easy. They had had some rough times, some close shaves with those who opposed Jesus. They must have looked into one another's faces to see if there were any telltale sign of guilt. They looked too into their own hearts, and wondered, Could it be me?

One man was sure it could not be he. Peter would rather die than betray his Master, and he was quick to say so. It came as a nasty shock to be told he would deny Jesus—and not once but three times. That hurt him. But he would prove his loyalty, he was sure of that.

So there was one man confident that it was not he who would betray Jesus, ten other men each wondering whether it possibly could be he. And the remaining man? Well, Judas knew who Jesus was talking about all right, but he kept his cool; not a flicker of guilt passed across his face. He did not betray himself, but would Jesus betray him? If Jesus had, Judas would have been a dead man; the others would have seen to that. But Jesus did not name him; rather, he gave him a place of honor and affection. He appealed to him with love, not anger. Up to the very last moment, Jesus still pleaded with Judas, and in such a way that the others would not realize just what was passing between them. Finally Jesus let him go, providing the way out himself; and Judas went out. The words of scripture put it so starkly: ". . . it was night."

Judas chose the darkness. He turned from the light. Why? Jesus had given the answer to that question quite early in his ministry, when a Jewish leader named Nicodemus had come secretly at night to talk to him. Jesus had talked about judgment and said, "This is the judgment, that the light has come into the world, and people loved darkness rather than light because their deeds were evil" (John 3:19).

Judas chose the darkness. It was his choice, even after seeing the light. How was it possible? Yet it happened. He accepted the bread from the one who was "the bread of life" and still went out into the night, to his own destruction.

What about us? Could we ever betray Jesus by our words and actions? Do we ever willfully turn our backs on him? We are privileged to share in the "breaking of bread"—called by various names by different groups of Christians, but the name doesn't really matter. We all come by invitation to the Lord's table to receive the tokens of his love for us. But it is so easy to take it for granted, to take it lightly, to take it when we are deliberately going against all that it represents. We may be dressed in our Sunday best, saying all the right words, looking the part—but what is really going on inside us? As we leave the place of communion, are we in effect doing as Judas did and going out into the night, into the darkness?

In the Book of Common Prayer of the Church of England the conditions for receiving Holy Communion are most clearly laid out: "Ye who do truly and earnestly repent you of your sins, and are in love and charity with your neighbors, and intend to lead a new life, following the commandments of God, and walking from henceforth in his holy ways; Draw near with faith . . . ." When you look at these conditions, and look at yourself, dare you come?

Can any of us say we are fit to come? A friend of mine was discussing this very point with me recently. She said, "There are times when I know I am in the wrong frame of mind, and yet what would other people think if I did not go up to communion? I know too that when I am at outs with everything and everybody, then I need it more than ever."

I could see what my friend meant, for this has been my own experience as well. Yet I take heart when I remember that Jesus offered the bread to Judas as well as the others. It was the offer of love. If Judas had been open to it, maybe he would not have gone out into the night. But it seems that his heart was hardened, his mind was made up. While we do recognize our frailty, while we are still open, there is hope.

The self-confident Peter and the not-so-sure ten, all let Jesus down later for a variety of reasons but not hardness of heart. Their hearts were still with Jesus, and they could know again the joy of being with him, belonging to him, being sent out to serve him, and so can we. So take heart! "Draw near with faith!" For the one who is "the bread of life" will sustain us and strengthen us for our journey through life, wherever that journey takes us.

Yet there is another condition. In receiving "the bread of life," we are then bound to one another as fellow travelers. For Jesus says, "I give you a new commandment, that you love one another. Just as I have loved you, you also should love one another."

Not easy, is it? Loving all the others. I don't suppose it was easy for the friends in the upper room. After all, they were a very mixed bunch. They even suspected one another of treachery; they were not absolutely certain of the next man, even though they had been together for three years. As I look around "the church," whether in my own congregation or at any gatherings of fellow Christians, and see those who join with me at the Lord's table, I sometimes wonder about some of them. *Can they be trusted? Do they really belong to the Lord? Do I have to love them?* The first two questions are not mine to ask or reply to, but the answer to the third question, *Do I have to love them?* is inescapable. Jesus commands me to love them.

I want to question his command, "Lord, you don't know them. They are so irritating and infuriating. They insist on their own way all the time. They get on my nerves!" Jesus says, "Just as I have loved you, you also should love one another." I really would prefer not to! I was complaining bitterly one day to a colleague about someone whom I was finding most difficult to get along with, and I said rather crossly, "The trouble is, I don't even like him." To which my friend replied with a smile, "You don't have to like him, Margaret, but you have to love him!"

Why should I? Why should I, indeed—except for the fact that Jesus loves me and commands me to love wholeheartedly regardless of how I feel about various individuals? Why should I? So that it will be evident that I belong to him. That is the proof that is looked for in me.

Put like that, it's quite simple and straightforward, but then the most important things usually are, aren't they?

Chapter 10 ⟶

One way only
John 14

WHY IS IT that when the world crashes about our ears, when everything we had planned on falls apart and we are in absolute confusion and despair, there is always some bright soul who slaps us on the back and says, "Don't get worried and upset!" Of course they are trying to be helpful, to calm us down and cheer us up, but somehow those words, and others in similar vein, only make matters worse. The bright-eyed, smiling friend is likely to get his smile and words stuffed down his throat—which may in itself prove a more therapeutic exercise for us than the words of the would-be helper!

The friends of Jesus had every reason to be worried and upset. Jesus had been telling them he was about to go away and leave them. It was pretty clear to them that the net was closing in, that those who were out to get him were in a very strong position. What was more, Jesus had just told them that one of their number would betray him and that Peter would deny he even knew him. What a prospect! All their hopes were dashed; everything loomed so large and frightening; and the one person whom they depended upon was leaving. Jesus urged them to go on believing in God and to believe in him. He told them he was going on ahead to prepare the way for them and promised to return again. He assured them that they would realize the truth of his promises and would be able to see the way ahead themselves.

Thomas jumped in with both feet. He challenged Jesus bluntly: "Lord, we do not know where you are going. How can we know the way?" Good point! Can you imagine setting out on a journey which is not even on the map and trying to get to the right spot? You wouldn't know where to start from, which path to follow. It is only when we know the destination that we can travel with any hope. We can then use our maps, ask people who have been there before, and take the right bearings. But a journey into the unknown—it sounds more like a huge gamble, with only a million-to-one chance of being remotely on the right road.

Life does seem, for most people, a huge gamble. It has too many possibilities. There are many attractive roads that so easily turn out to be dead ends, exciting and enticing highways that can land us in real trouble. There are endless conflicting views, with so many and varied claims by personalities and organizations to be *the* way that it seems sheer luck whether we make any real progress in life. We end by changing direction over and over again, going around in ever-decreasing circles until we flop down with exhaustion, having gotten nowhere—fast!

Jesus was unperturbed by Thomas's questioning. "I am the way, and the truth, and the life," he said, and continued, "No one comes to the Father except through me. If you know me, you will know my Father also. From now on you do know him and have seen him."

This "explanation" was just too much for another of the friends, Philip, to take. All this talk was so confusing. What he wanted was to see the Father; that would solve all his problems. Jesus gently yet firmly reproached Philip for asking such a question. Surely after all this time, Philip must have realized who Jesus was. Could it be that Philip just had not grasped that Jesus and God are one? If only people would grasp that and believe it, then they could ask anything in the name of Jesus, and God would grant it, because Jesus and his Father are one and the same—God. Not only this, but the Spirit would come to be the Helper, and the Spirit would reveal the truth about God—God the Father, God the Son, and God the Holy Spirit.

The friends were still muddled and confused, still questioning. If what Jesus said were so, they wanted to know, why were they—

and not the rest of the world—privileged to receive the truth? Here they were, a few ordinary men, and out there was a world that contained learned people, powerful people, religious people. So why was the greatest truth of all given to a small group in an upstairs room rather than to the world in a blaze of glory? The answer was that the truth was revealed to those who would obey Jesus because they loved him. They would get all the help they would need; it would all be made clear, it would all drop into place because the Holy Spirit would be their teacher, and the wisdom the Holy Spirit would impart to them would be the wisdom of God.

"Do not let your hearts be troubled, and do not let them be afraid." I read those words many times, most often to people who are at their wits' end, in an extremity of grief and pain, following the death of a loved one. Those words of Jesus are the words I choose to speak to those who mourn, those who stand at a graveside, who look into the darkness of the earth and see only despair. I expect some who hear the words think me a fool to read them. They would, if they were not so polite, throw them back at me and challenge me to prove them. Yet I continue to read them and believe them. I offer these words not as sentimental idealism but as assurance and hope. I point to Jesus, who with arms open wide stands as the eternal signpost—the signpost to God, the way provided by God, and the giver of the Holy Spirit, who will help them along the way to God.

Father, Son, and Holy Spirit—how many books have been written, lectures delivered, sermons preached on the great theological truths of the Holy Trinity! How many Sunday school teachers have struggled to explain, perhaps with the aid of a shamrock leaf, what "three in one and one in three" is all about! One local preacher confided to me some time ago, "I dread being asked to preach on Trinity Sunday. It is beyond me." Yes, it is beyond me to explain—let others more learned and well-trained in theological exposition do that. The best explanation I have found is that contained in the *Family Worship* book, published by Church Pastoral

Aid Society (CPAS), where, in place of the Creed, three questions are asked, and three answers given.

Do you believe in God? I believe in God the Father who made me and all the world.

Do you believe in Jesus Christ? I believe in Jesus Christ, the Son of God who came to this earth to be my Savior. He died for my sins on the cross, rose again from the dead, ascended to the Father in heaven and will come again in his glory as Judge of all people.

Do you believe in the Holy Spirit? I believe in the Holy Spirit whom God gives to all who trust in Christ. The Holy Spirit makes me more like Jesus, guides and strengthens me in my daily life, and helps me to serve God in the family of the Church.

Father, Son, and Holy Spirit, available for you and for me—that is the glorious truth, the good news for the little people and the big people, the household names and those who make up the unknown and unsung, the wise and the foolish. And all we have to do to know Father, Son, and Holy Spirit is to trust the one who is the way, the truth, and the life, to love and to obey him—just that!

Knowing the Trinity is not something to be worked out only in the mind (although we do well to try, for we need to grapple with theological truth), but we must clothe our understanding with the flesh of experience. What matters is that we live it out in love and obedience. If we will do this, we are given a very special gift, the gift of peace. Jesus gave peace as his parting gift to those who would count themselves among his friends. It is not a peace that will allow us to shut out the world, its troubles or its joys. This peace will not relieve us of the ups and downs that are common to all. It will not contain us in a germ-free bubble, for we have to live in the world; we are part and parcel of humanity, not living on our own personal desert island. It is the peace of God, the *shalom*, the wholeness of being at one with God, knowing that past, present, and future are safe because he holds us and takes us through it all.

To that little band of frightened men Jesus gave the precious gift of his *shalom*, so that when they were worried and upset, they could release their fears and anxieties and be at peace. They would have loved to have remained in that upper room with the Lord and Master forever—what peace that would have been! Yet Jesus moved on immediately: "Rise, let us be on our way." They had to leave that place that would always hold such special memories, where they had been washed and fed, where they had shared in such sacred moments with Jesus, and go out into the world—a tough, harsh, brutal world. But they would carry with them the *shalom* of God. It would never be taken away from them. It would remain forever.

Often, in a place of beauty and quietness, when I experience the presence of the Lord in a special way, I long to remain there forever, undisturbed by the ugliness and noise of the world. Within the warmth of Christian fellowship, perhaps in a house group in our parish or at a conference of like-minded people living in a community based on Jesus, I would like to close the gate on ordinary life, everyday life. I must admit I have a selfish and cowardly nature which, when I am perhaps at my happiest, makes me want to say to the rest of the world, "I'm doing all right, thank you. Just take care of yourselves!" Why should I leave my peace and go out into a society that well may go on all right without me? Why ask for trouble?

Perhaps that close band of friends in the upper room would not have expressed themselves as I have, but I am pretty sure they felt the same! Yet they had to go out—and go out with confidence, secure in the love and power of God, given by Jesus, and with that bonus package of peace. They had to go out knowing they could turn to God at any time for help in Jesus' name. They ventured out with the assurance, even though they had not begun to grasp its implications, that they were going out to do works even greater than those Jesus had already done.

Those who have taken the promises of Jesus and acted upon them have found them to be gloriously true. Jesus himself never moved outside Palestine; he had addressed crowds numbering only thousands, healed only a fraction of a vast multitude of diseases, dealt with only a limited variety of problems. The world he lived in here on earth was small and restricted; it had yet to explode in all directions. The friends of Jesus in the last two thousand years have shared his good news with millions, using every modern means, not least the printed word in thousands of languages. Think too of radio and television. One broadcast can reach more people than most preachers could address preaching twenty-four hours a day for a hundred years.

Men and women have gone to the four corners of the earth to bring Jesus to others, and many, through dedicated medical care, have brought healing and new life to countless people. Day by day the barriers are broken; new technology and skills make miracles an every-minute affair. Those who go out today in the name of Jesus are backed up by every modern means of communication. They have the tools, the know-how, and the advantage of two thousand years of growing experience. Jesus is the same "yesterday and today and forever" (Heb. 13:8), but he is not static. He is alive and active, moving in today's world with power, using the same basic material, though—men and women who know and love him and who go out and share him.

For me too comes the call to get up and go. To be refreshed by Jesus in quietness and beauty or to experience his cleansing and renewing in fellowship puts me back on my feet, so that I may be pushed out into the world. Those words of Jesus "Rise, let us be on our way" are spoken to me also—twenty-first-century middle-aged woman that I am! There's work to be done; there's a world out there. His words come to you too if you count yourself a friend of his. There's work for you to do—so on your feet! Like all the followers of Jesus, past, present, and to come, we go out with his words ringing in our ears: "If in my name you ask me for anything, I will do it. . . . My peace I give to you. . . . Do not . . . be afraid."

Chapter 11

Multiply or die
John 15:1-17

FOR THREE YEARS Jesus had shared his life with a small group of men. Each was called into a unique relationship with him. They were disciples—learners, students, pupils, apprentices—specially selected for the biggest job in history, to carry the good news into every part of the world. They were the A-team, the Number One group. If they failed, what chance was there?

Jesus had spent those three years teaching, preaching, and healing. He had addressed himself to individuals and to the crowds, but with this small group he had shared the deepest truths, had spent time developing the teaching and giving them insight concerning the kingdom of God. Three years—the time required for a student in the U.K. today to obtain a degree, from entering university or college to graduation day. Three years for Jesus' pupils to graduate and to begin to produce results.

The last term was running out fast; the final examinations loomed ahead. One disciple had already dropped out; now there were only eleven. What were their chances? What of the Master? He had to hand on his life's work to the team. Would they prove worthy of the last three years? Did they have "stickability"?

Jesus had very little time left for final instructions. He spelled out the position they were in, the options open. He chose as his illustration one of the most common visual aids around—the vine. It was grown all over Palestine. Everywhere one looked there were vines growing, some producing well and giving a tremendous return, while many had gone wild, producing only leaves, taking over the ground, taking goodness out of the soil but worthless, fit only for a bonfire.

The image of the vine would have been well known to those men who had listened so intently to Jesus. Israel had been described by the prophets of old as an empty vine—active, rampant but unproductive. Sadly this description had proved so in Israel's history. Yet the vine was still the symbol of Jewish imagery; the desire of God's people was to be like a fruitful vine. God had dealt severely with his people, and still they went on showing the signs of life yet producing nothing.

So Jesus uses the picture of the vine and proclaims in God's name—"I AM"—that he is the true vine and his pupils the branches. There are two essential requirements. The first is to be united with Jesus, to be part of him. That means sharing his life, being at one with him, obeying his commands, allowing his life to flow through them. If they think they can go it alone, doing their own thing, they will be as useless as a broken-off branch, for when the branch is broken, the life is severed and the branch dries up, rots away, or is burned—destruction is its destiny.

It is not enough, though, merely to belong, to be a passenger. The whole point of the vine branch is the fruit it bears. To bear fruit, the vine has to be cared for, vigorously pruned back, protected, and fed; the fruit-bearing branches are valuable indeed! Nothing pleases any gardener more than to see the fruit hanging from the branches. The gardener is proud of his or her work and enjoys the admiration of others; the fruit has brought the gardener glory and is proof that the labor has been blessed by success. The gardener has plenty to sing and cheer about. Harvest time is party time, the celebrations go on and on. . . . And then it is time to prune, to build up, to look forward to another bumper harvest. The cycle continues.

Two thousand years ago the symbol of the vine would have meant much more than it does for most of us today in our industrialized society. Yet we can see exactly what it means. "Business is business," whether measured by the milk yield, the fruit crop, or the assembly line producing the latest in washing machines or cars. The figures determine whether the sole proprietorship or the multinational corporation stays in business or gets the chop. What matters is not whether the operation is a happy setup, the premises are good, the workers are content, but whether there are results. In soccer terms, it is goals in the back of the net that count!

Of course we know this reality; it's a fact of life. But have we grasped the fact of our Christian life? The same rules apply—production or destruction. Jesus says so!

Where does that leave you and me? The first question we must ask is whether we are part of Jesus, united in his body. Is his life flowing through us? "Do I really belong?" There is only one way we can be united with him— by accepting him as our Master, Savior, and Lord. But what about the other bit—bearing fruit, producing results, showing a profit? It sounds rather commercial, rather too businesslike, but shouldn't we be businesslike in God's service?

In preparing a paper for a conference, titled "Hindrances to Mission," I listed all the things I thought hindered the mission of the church. I finished up with a lengthy list, including lack of training, shortage of time, insufficient funding, preoccupation with personal ambition, and plain apathy! Yet as I looked at my list I realized that these were but the symptoms; the basic problems were unbelief and disobedience. Within our churches there are many who are unbelievers. They are paper members, pew-sitters, meeting-attenders, supporters in various ways but unbelievers for all that.

Once by way of illustration in a sermon, I quoted how many Christians there are in the world, intending to encourage our congregation and show them they were part of something big! One man came up to me as I stood at the door after the service. "You know that figure you quoted this morning? Are they all really Christians or just church members?" I confessed the figure was probably derived from membership returns. "But who would you say was a Christian then?" he persisted, and then added, "Would you say I was one?" I looked at him and said, "You should know whether you are or not." He did not reply, but since that conversation he has opened up much more. He is, I believe, on the road to faith, because he had to question where he himself stood with Jesus.

Yes, unbelief is unfortunately all too common in our churches, and perhaps those of us who stand in the pulpit week by week must bear the blame. We have assumed too much from counting attendance or figures on the roll rather than challenging those who are within our membership with the black-and-white facts of the gospel. We have allowed people to believe that they can enter the kingdom of Heaven through good will, by having their names on a membership list, participating in church events, or clocking in to worship Sunday after Sunday.

And what of those who are Christians, who have a personal faith? Are they bearing fruit or producing a good show of greenery? Are you producing any fruit? What do you have to show for yourself?

Jesus spoke very directly to his group of pupils. If they did not go on to bear fruit, his work would have been in vain. They had to multiply or die. Thank God, they went on to bear fruit. The church grew by leaps and bounds; the frontiers were pushed out; the good news was shared. The disciples were obedient, they did as they were told. They willingly underwent the discipline and hardships, so that Jesus was honored and accepted. Then others took up the challenge, and so they carried on through the centuries, bearing fruit. The price was high, but they paid it gladly.

The price is still high. Jesus demands our obedience, total obedience. When we obey, we too will bear fruit. It will cost us everything, but in exchange what do we get? To be part of Jesus—his body. To share in his glory and his joy. And we graduate from being servants to being friends; that makes all the difference in the world.

Part of my work when I was appointed broadcasting officer for the York Diocese included serving the Archbishop of York, who, for the first eight years of my appointment, was Dr. Stuart Blanch. I did many radio interviews with him and attended a multitude of press conferences and other events. I was also made deaconess by him in York Minister and promised to obey him "in all things lawful and honest." It was a great pleasure to serve him; whatever he asked me to do, I did gladly, not just because he was the archbishop but out of great personal affection for him. He was "the boss," but more than that he was my friend, and I could turn to him at any time. He was concerned for me as me, and not just as a broadcasting officer or a deaconess. To serve him was a privilege; to know his friendship was and is a joy.

Jesus offers us that same relationship with him—not just the privilege of service but the joy of being his friend. Surely that is worth everything, bearing in mind the awful alternative?

Chapter 12 ⟿

You have been warned

John 15:18–16:15

T HE WORLD is wary of those who suggest that there is an alternative way of ordering society. New ideas can pose a threat to the established leadership, and people who claim to have discovered a way of life that will radically alter both the social structures and individuals are to be viewed with suspicion. Such people can prove dangerous for they do not conform to accepted ways. It is thought better to remove them from the scene, so that life can go on as normal, as dictated by the powers that be and as life has always been.

Jesus was such a person. He challenged every stratum of society—individually, politically, socially, and in the most tender area of all, the religious life of his day. He trod on the toes of the Establishment until gradually embarrassment turned to disapproval, then to hatred. Time and time again, attempts were made to get rid of him, to destroy Jesus and his message. Such attempts were made on those who followed him; they too were dangerous and posed a threat, so they must be eliminated.

Jesus tells his friends plainly what the situation is: "If the world hates you, be aware that it hated me before it hated you." He goes further, with an even more painful announcement: "They will put you out of the synagogues. Indeed, an hour is coming when those who kill you will think that by doing so they are offering worship to God." Not a pleasant prospect, to be hated by the world, by those who had no time for religion but also by those who should have been a support, their fellow Jews. What chance was their survival against such overwhelming odds?

71

The friends of Jesus would soon experience what he had warned them about. They would undergo persecution from many quarters, not least from those who were God-fearing, religious people, and from their leaders. Perhaps that would be the hardest to bear, to be hated by those who should have realized who Jesus was and received him with joy.

It has never changed. The words of Jesus ring down through the centuries: "They will do this because they have not known the Father or me." Anne Arnott, in her account of the life of John Bunyan, *He Shall with Giants Fight* (Kingsway, 1985), describes the dreadful persecution Bunyan endured from those who thought they were doing God's will in their treatment of that holy man who gave us *Pilgrim's Progress*. She reminds us that he was "ever to be remembered for his heroic stand as a prisoner of conscience whose one desire was to witness for his Lord."

There have been and still are many prisoners of conscience witnessing for their Lord in spite of hatred and persecution. Many have risked and even given their lives—good, saintly men and women, whose only crime has been to serve Jesus Christ. People like Archbishop Janani Luwum of Uganda, murdered, as were so many Ugandan Christians during the Amin regime; like many Christian leaders in South Africa, such as Archbishop Desmond Tutu, who suffered continual harassment; like Bishop Dehqani-Tafti of Iran, whose son was murdered and who narrowly escaped with his own life. And what of the thousands of nameless Christians in places like southern Sudan, Pakistan, and Indonesia, suffering today because of their faith?

Consider the situation in Northern Ireland, where Christians, both Catholics and Protestants, who work for peace and understanding based on the love of Jesus are misunderstood, rejected, and often in danger from those they try to help. In mainland Britain, many ministers and their families, particularly in the cities, are victims of violence. A friend of mine, a vicar in Hull, arrived late for a meeting. He apologized and explained, "Sorry I'm late, but we were burgled yet again last night, and the vicarage was vandalized." Church buildings are often the subject of vandalism, their furnishings destroyed, defaced, or stolen. Those who speak out in the media, especially on moral issues, are constantly subjected to abusive telephone calls and letters. These are just some examples of what happens when people are prepared to stand up and be counted as followers of Jesus.

In the Church of England baptism service, the child—or it may also be an adult—is signed with the sign of the cross and then charged with these words: "Do not be ashamed to confess the faith of Christ crucified. Fight valiantly under the banner of Christ, against sin, the world, and the devil, and continue his faithful soldier and servant to the end of your life." Following Jesus is no easy option, for Christians swim against the tide; sin, the world, and the devil will try to pull them back and under.

With so much pressure, what chance have we got? How can we cope? The fact of the matter is that we cannot cope. We cannot win the battle on our own, not even the strongest of us. But help is at hand from the Holy Spirit, the one who is "the Helper."

For the friends of Jesus, the promise of the Holy Spirit would not take away the fear, the sadness, and the confusion of that moment. So much was happening to them; everything was in turmoil; all they knew was that Jesus was leaving them. They would be alone in an alien world and, if anything, things would get worse. As yet the Holy Spirit was beyond their experience or understanding. There was a limit to what they could take in at that time. Jesus wanted to tell them so much more, but he knew they could not take it: "I still have many things to say to you, but you cannot bear them now." So he just reminds them again that help will come. Then they will understand; they will be given the power to rise above fear and hatred, above death itself.

In time, those friends would begin to understand what Jesus had been telling them all the time he was with them. Gradually they would become aware of the meaning of things that had happened during their three years "on the road" with him. Things that puzzled them would suddenly become gloriously clear, and the memories of the past would become entrances into a totally new understanding of the kingdom of God. But all this was in the future; they had to live through the present.

There are times when life does not make sense, when we cannot understand what is happening to us. Part of us cries out for the answers, wanting to know what will happen tomorrow, next week, next year. There are those who turn to fortune-tellers—to those they hope will unravel the future for them. How sad and how dangerous this is! What good would it do to know, even if it were possible to know? When, early in his ministry, Jesus talked to the people on the hillside about being anxious over what was to come, he said, "So do not worry about tomorrow, for tomorrow will bring worries of its own" (Matt. 6:34). In other words, live one day at a time. And as my vicar is always telling me when I push toward what I think ought to be done this very minute and which actually is perhaps days or even weeks ahead: "Today's trouble is enough for today." Help will come. It will be given when we need it, and when the time is right we will begin to understand. Then everything will fall into place, for the Helper who Jesus promised his friends would come, has come, and he will lead you and me into all the truth we need, at the right time.

I find it hard to wait. I want to know everything *now!* That is part of my very impatient nature. And yet how gently Jesus deals with me, reminding me that it is in his time and not mine that I will understand the inevitability of waiting—not because he wants to withhold things from me but because he knows me and knows my limits. Archbishop William Temple expresses this idea sensitively in his *Readings in St. John's Gospel* (Macmillan, 1940): "The disciple is not to clamour for the solution of perplexities or for intellectual mastery of divine mysteries. What knowledge he has in this realm is his because the Spirit has declared it to him; and for the Spirit's declaration he must wait." Wise words to the impatient, puzzled, "let's get up and go" disciple, who says, "I want to know, and I want to know *now*."

Maybe I am beginning to learn to wait, although rather

impatiently. The fact that I know the Lord is here; that his Spirit is with us, assures me that everything will be all right in spite of the way it may seem at this moment. Waiting is hard, but the answers are worth waiting for!

Chapter 13 ⌒

. . . But it was worth it!
John 16:16-33

I CAME TO motherhood somewhat late—in fact I was thirty and in the eyes of the medical profession at that time "at risk" because of my age and various complications I developed during pregnancy. The baby was overdue, and so steps were taken to induce the birth. It was mid-January in one of the coldest, snowiest years on record; the hospital was one of the oldest in the country; the pipes froze; the heating went off; and at one point the lighting failed. Going into labor in that situation was anything but pleasant, and the labor was long and protracted. Finally in the middle of the night our son was born, a forceps delivery. It had been difficult, dangerous, and painful, but nothing could equal the sound of that baby crying as he came into the world and the congratulatory words of the doctor, "You have a son." What a thrill to have a bundle placed in my arms, the bundle that was Julian Peter Cundiff. Later, wheeled back into the ward of sleeping women, I was so excited that I woke the woman in the next bed and proudly announced, "I've had a baby." "Have you, luv, I am pleased," was her reply! By early morning when the tea came round I had written a pile of letters, filled in all the cards that were to go to relatives and friends, and I felt I had the energy left to climb Everest!

Three years later our daughter, Alison, arrived. She had the sense to arrive in May, in a newly opened, ultra-modern hospital, and at tea time! But the thrill was just the same, following an anxious time, though thankfully not quite as bad as with our son. Any mother will recognize in what I have described her own experience of "before" and "after"—the anxiety, the pain, the struggle, all forgotten in the joy of birth. Every mother feels at the moment of delivery that she is the only person in the world to have accomplished so much. Even winning a gold medal in the Olympics could not be more exhilarating.

Jesus used that illustration of childbirth to explain to his friends what they would have to go through in the next few days. He knew that ahead of them lay great sadness, suffering, and fear. The pain for him would be so much more, but he had the assurance of his Father, whom he knew and trusted. Even though he shrank from what was to come, he accepted it because he knew it was the way to life and glory. If he could have, he would have gone through the suffering of his friends too. But like a woman in childbirth, each person must go through it alone; there is no other way. When a new life comes into the world, it comes through pain to birth, to joy. The Jewish people used the picture of childbirth to describe the coming of the new age, when the messiah would appear. They knew he would burst through the agony barrier, gloriously bringing in his kingdom. Yet they did not realize that the time of delivery had arrived, that it was upon them; they lost out on the triumph of God.

Sadness and joy are interwoven. The pain of parting, for those who love each other, is so intense, but what joy is there to compare with that of reunion? One of the young men from our church, a sailor, served in the Falklands. I well remember the sadness and anxiety we all felt as he went from us and the agonizing time, particularly for his family and his fiancée, when it was announced that his ship had been sunk, and it was not yet known who had survived. Nothing could describe those hours of waiting, the blackness and despair we all felt. But then came the telephone call that confirmed he had been picked up. He was alive! There were plenty more tears shed, but this time they were tears of joy, and there were even more as he came home to one of the best parties ever. For me the delight was to be even greater a year later, when I assisted at the wedding of Terry and Judith. In the vestry I was gathered into the arms of the handsome young sailor in uniform, proudly wearing his Falklands medal. The first woman he kissed as a married man was the deaconess—closely followed by the bride! Yes, life is made up of sorrow and joy, anxiety and relief, agony and ecstasy.

Jesus used many homely illustrations to explain great spiritual truths. Every preacher and teacher does the same. Examples drawn from what we know and understand lead us to see beyond and will shed new light on something that confuses us. Then the time comes when we need no illustration, for the light has dawned; we understand the truth. Jesus had often spoken in parables, so that the light would filter in through the darkness. Soon there would be no more need for illustration. The great visual aids of all time would be seen—the cross, which would speak forever of the unlimited love of God, and the empty tomb, which would speak of the power and victory of love. The Holy Spirit would come in love and power and fill men and women with the spiritual force that they would need for the new age.

But this was still in the future. Those friends of Jesus had yet to discover the power of the Holy Spirit, but for now their questions were answered, even the unspoken ones. Jesus had looked into their hearts and answered them. They now knew that everything Jesus had told them was true. They were convinced.

His friends were convinced now, but Jesus knew that soon they would doubt, they would run away, they would fail—but only for a time. Gently he warned them what would happen. He knew they would run away and fail, but when it happened he wanted them to remember that he would know, he would understand, he would still love them, and they could be at peace, knowing that everything was under control. Suffering lay ahead, but Jesus had already won the victory. The world would do its worst, but nothing could separate them from him or from his Father, who was their Father.

Later on a man named Saul, a man very much of the world, feared by those who followed Jesus because of his persecution campaign against Christians, would become a follower of Jesus. He would himself experience hatred, persecution, and great suffering, yet he would become the greatest influence ever for Jesus. Saul the persecutor became Paul the great missionary and apostle. He eventually took the good news of Jesus to Rome. His letters have been the means of coming to know Jesus for countless men and women, even in our own century. Men and women have been inspired to go on following Jesus in spite of the pain, the persecution, the scorn of the world. Paul could triumphantly say, "Who will separate us from the love of Christ? Will hardship, or distress, or persecution, or famine, or nakedness, or peril, or sword? . . . No, in all these things we are more than conquerors through him who loved us" (Rom. 8:35, 37).

Paul put into words what millions have discovered to be true, that Jesus has won the victory. Many have gone to their death with the words of Jesus ringing in their ears: "In the world you face persecution. But take courage; I have conquered the world!"

For most of us, the suffering we have to go through will be nothing compared with the suffering of those who have given their lives, who have died heroically as martyrs. Yet we are all called to suffer. We all experience our little deaths in the world. We all plumb the depths at times—maybe through fear, depression, doubt, ridicule, snide remarks, the cold shoulder, rejection by those who we hoped would have understood. The words of Jesus come to renew our courage and hope. They rally us to our feet; they beckon us home: "I have conquered the world!" Secure in that knowledge, what have we to fear?

Chapter 14 ⟶

Listen—he's praying for you
John 17

NOW IT WAS TIME to move out from the intimate meeting place, away from that room that had enclosed them in love and fellowship, where they had experienced for the last time the joy of being together, sharing a meal. That meal would be reenacted until the end of time, with its sharing of heart and mind and spirit. Jesus had shared with his friends in the deepest possible way. He had sought to prepare and equip them for what lay ahead. Soon he would be leaving them; the future would lie with that small group of bewildered and anxious men.

As they rose to their feet to go out into the world's arena, to "go public," Jesus stopped, lifted his eyes to heaven, and began to pray. I can feel the atmosphere; I can see those friends of Jesus with their eyes on him, silently watching and waiting as they realize that they are witnessing not just a man at prayer but a Father and Son bound together in love—God the Father and God the Son.

To read the seventeenth chapter of John's Gospel is to stand listening with those friends of Jesus in silence, in wonder. It is also to be enfolded in the security of love. It is a glimpse of glory that is now and is to be, a glory that we share in.

"[Jesus] looked up to heaven . . . ." Perhaps those who stood and watched him remembered his standing outside the tomb of his friend Lazarus, when he prayed then that the glory of God might be seen as the dead man was brought back to life. They would have remembered how immediately that glory had been seen as Lazarus emerged from the grave, alive, strong, free. God's glory was powerfully seen as death was conquered, flung aside in defeat like the rejected grave clothes.

"[Jesus] looked up to heaven . . . ." The cross lay ahead, but so did the glorious victory. The thanksgiving had already begun as Father and Son met together. Jesus had shown the glory of God from the beginning of his life on earth, and he would leave the world in the blaze of God's glory. He could say, "I glorified you on earth by finishing the work that you gave me to do." No wonder he had such a sense of completeness with his Father.

Perhaps we all know in a small way at times that sense of completeness when we successfully finish a job. It may be a very simple thing or an exhausting program that has drained us of our energy, taken all our time, strained us to the limits. Writing a book is a bit like that—it is for me, at any rate. The demands of a time schedule, burning the midnight oil, struggling to be able to put the right words on to the paper, coping with the irritation of interruptions when I am in the middle of something that is beginning to flow, and taking with a smile the remarks of well-meaning friends who do not see the point of the book anyway. Yet all is forgotten as the manuscript is handed over, the deadline met. Later, when the manuscript is actually a book on the shelves, bought and read, it is all worthwhile. There is a sense of achievement, the satisfaction of finishing the job, producing the work, and seeing the smile on the face of my editor!

I do not think it is irreverent to compare simple human endeavor with how Jesus must have felt as he met his deadline and knew his Father's pleasure. How did God feel? Do you ever wonder that? I can speak again only as a parent, remembering my children as youngsters. I recall the joy and the pleasure I felt as I saw my son, dark rings under the eyes from the long hours of study, because he had been poring over his books rather than out in the open air enjoying his fishing, waving his final essay in the air and saying, "Mum, it's finished!" Or my daughter proudly carrying in the cake she had made and iced for Christmas, announcing, "Look, it's finished. Do you like it?"

A book, an essay, a cake—all these very ordinary human accomplishments give me a taste of glory and point me to the one of whom John could write ". . . and we have seen his glory" (John 1:14).

Jesus and God were in complete harmony, and because of their relationship we can know God and so know eternal life. The word *know*, as in verse 3, has a much deeper meaning than simply acceptance of a truth, such as a knowing that two and two make four, or C-A-T spells cat. William Temple says, in *Readings in St. John's Gospel*:

> The word for "know" here is not that which stands for a grasp of truth; it is that which stands for personal acquaintance. Even in human friendships there is the constant delight of new discoveries by each in the character of the other. Eternity cannot be too long for our finite spirits to advance in knowledge of the infinite God.

In Jesus' prayer we see the Father-and-Son relationship, and we also see Jesus the representative, the "great high priest." He enters into his Father's presence on others' behalf too! As his friends listened to his prayer, they would suddenly become aware that Jesus was bringing them into his Father's presence, into that holy of holies. He presented them to his Father with joy and thanksgiving. He asked his Father to keep them safe. He asked his Father to protect them—not to take them out of the world but to keep them safe within it, so that they too might show his glory. Jesus had given his friends everything; now he entrusted them to his Father. His friends could never forget that prayer; it would be written on their hearts. And as Jesus prayed, it would bring them joy and peace and hope, even in the dark days ahead, even to the end of their lives.

What a unique privilege to be brought to God in prayer by Jesus! What assurance it must have given those friends that they, ordinary men, had been considered important enough, had been loved enough for Jesus to be concerned to the extent that he shared his concern for them with his Father. As the friends listened, they must have been filled with love for Jesus as they heard him pray for them. It must have imbued them with the determination to live out his prayer, to be the people he wanted them to be.

And Jesus didn't finish there. He went on, "I ask not only on behalf of these, but also on behalf of those who will believe in me through their word, that they may all be one." Do you realize for whom Jesus was praying then? Has it dawned on you whom he meant? Do you believe in Jesus? Have you come to know him, maybe through the witness of a friend or within a Christian family? after hearing a preacher, reading a book, seeing a film, or being faced with words of scripture on a poster? We come to know Jesus through the witness of others, through the faithfulness of generations. We are able to read the Word of God because of the faithful witnesses who wrote it. We read it in our own language because of the faithfulness of translators, printers, and distributors. We can hear God's word because of the faithfulness of those who have preached and proclaimed that word, who have shared the good news. We will never know this side of heaven how many links have been in the chain of our coming to know Jesus. For them and for us, for you and for me, Jesus prayed.

How do you feel, knowing that Jesus prayed for us to be one? It makes me want to do all I can to help answer his prayer. He prayed that you and I might be one, of the same mind and heart as he and as one another. I often hear people speak disparagingly about "ecumaniacs"—they pour cold water on schemes for Christian unity and refuse to be involved in acts of united witness and sharing. Yet Jesus prayed that we might all be one—not a uniformity so bland and colorless that it has no taste or use but the oneness Jesus and his Father enjoyed. We are to be one—"all be one" in Jesus Christ. And that includes being one with our Christian brothers and sisters of other cultures, colors, languages. We are to be so much at one with them that we would give our very lives for them.

We are called to be at one with those who are closest to us within the organizations of the church, the home groups, the fellowship meetings, with those who serve alongside us on the church council, the elders' meeting, or on one of the multitude of committees that are both the bane and blessing of church life. Perhaps here lies the greatest obstacle to our oneness. It is so difficult to be at one with those we rub shoulders with day in, day out—the rubbing along together can cause some very nasty friction burns! There is a tension born of being closely involved with one another in the church; we are each so sure we have all the answers and even *are* the answers! The problems arise as other people think exactly the same about themselves! We are all guilty; we are given more to individuality than to oneness with the others.

The friends of Jesus were just the same as we are. They had to live and work together. They were a varied bunch of individuals; oneness did not come easily to them. There were petty quarrels, misunderstandings, hidden resentments. There were flare-ups, party spirit, the desire for one-upmanship. Human nature does not change! And the church is full of human nature in the raw!

Sadly, how we behave toward one another is seen not only by those within the church but by those outside. Our witness is not to being all one but to being fragmented and divided. Sometimes the verdict of the world is not "See how these Christians love one another" but "See how they hate one another." Because of the intensity of our feelings, which we believe are one hundred percent right, we easily hurt one another. And those hurts can fester and destroy, unless we allow the one who prayed so passionately for us to deal with them. To be all one in Jesus is no easy matter; it will cost us dearly. But however high the price, it will never approach the price Jesus paid for us to be at one with him and his Father.

At a service in York Minster in 1986, Catholics, led by Cardinal Basil Hume, joined with Anglicans in commemorating the four hundredth anniversary of the martyrdom of Margaret Clitherow, a York butcher's wife killed by other Christians for refusing to renounce her Catholic faith. The then Archbishop of York Dr. John Habgood said in his sermon:

Our religious impulses have to be brought again and again
to the place of forgiveness. The things that can so easily
distort religious commitment—pride and fear and self-
seeking and humbug—have to be offered up and given
back to us by God as faith and hope and love. The lust for
certainty, the need to be right, the wish to dominate and
control, have to be brought to the cross of Christ and
endure the searching gaze of one who died helpless and
forsaken. The religious fortress mentality which keeps us
separated from one another and ultimately tempts us to
make martyrs of one another has to be broken down.

Jesus' prayer was that we might know the joy of being one with
him and with one another and witness by our lives the reality of
that oneness. Will we ever all be one? I believe the answer lies not
in great schemes, although it is right that we should continually strive
for unity with all the Christian traditions, but in learning to love
unreservedly our fellow Christians in the local situation. When
people in the world around see the Jesus-quality of love in your
life and mine, then there's a chance they may listen to what we
have to say.

When Jesus had finished praying, he and his friends walked
down the valley, across the brook Kidron, and into a place where
they had spent many happy times together. It was a garden—a
place of peace and quiet, a place in which to enjoy the company
of friends. It would be anything but peaceful and quiet this time.
It was here that the paths of Jesus and his friends would part company, and the garden would go into the record books as the place
where Jesus was betrayed by a friend. The name of the garden
was Gethsemane.

Chapter 15

What sort of man could do that?

John 18:1-11

THE ACCOUNT of Jesus' arrest in the garden of Gethsemane contains elements that puzzle me. There are features that are hard to understand. It is like trying to fit one of those wooden puzzle balls together without having the small central piece. Those relevant features were probably so obvious to those who were there at the time that no one thought it necessary to record them. After all, everybody knew the situation at the time; and would they have thought that two thousand years later people would be reading of the arrest of Jesus and puzzling over a very simple point?

Yet each time I read of the arrest, these questions arise in my mind. Why did the authorities have to go to all the trouble of paying an informer to betray Jesus? After all, Jesus was well known. He did not go around in disguise; he did not hide away. He was not surrounded by a private army.

Why did they send so many armed men, both Roman soldiers and temple guards, to pick up one unarmed man? It seems to me a very involved way of dealing with a simple matter. But then I wasn't there! What is clear is that it happened the way the New Testament said it did. All four Gospel accounts record it. Obviously since the event was seen through different eyes, some minor points differ, but all Gospels record the place, the manner of arrest, and the events that followed.

Jesus was with his friends in the garden, a place they often visited to enjoy, to wander in, to talk together in a pleasant spot, just as most of us enjoy walking in our own or other people's gardens, strolling around, relaxing in natural beauty. Then suddenly the place was full of armed men, with lanterns and torches. Perhaps they were armed because they were afraid of Jesus; after all, they would know he had the power to work miracles—there was plenty of evidence of those. Could it be that he was possessed of great personal strength, more than any other man? Did he carry a secret weapon? Did he even have a secret army that would spring out of the darkness to protect him? These were all possibilities that must be prepared for. On the other hand, hearing their approach, Jesus might flee from them and hide. He knew the area well, and there had been times before when he had seemed almost to melt away from sight. So lanterns and torches would be needed to aid their search. One thing was sure: They meant to find him and overpower him; that is why so many men went out; why they carried with them weapons, torches, and lanterns. They were ready for anything; they had all possibilities covered—it was a military operation.

Jesus could, of course, try to pass himself off as someone else— those loose eastern garments would aid his disguise; in the rush he would look like any other Jewish male around thirty years old. Ah, but they had thought about that one as well! Judas, one of his closest friends, had agreed to point Jesus out to them, to approach him. Then it would be a simple matter quickly to overpower him, tie him up, and take him away.

What actually happened was all very different from what they had expected—so different, it threw them completely. Jesus asked them who they were looking for, and when they replied, "Jesus of Nazareth," he calmly announced, "I am he."

Their response was strange in the extreme, for they moved back and fell on the ground. Think about that! All those armed men falling back and over and Jesus just standing there unarmed, unhidden. What was it in his manner that made them afraid? Could it have been they suddenly realized that here was no ordinary man? Here was someone who could wipe the lot of them off the face of the earth if he wanted to. Here was the one who spoke like God, using the name of God, "I AM." In a modern expression, he put "the fear of God" in them!

Jesus just stood there. His only request was that the friends he had with him be allowed to leave. After all, they were not needed. But Peter was all for making a fight of it and hit out wildly, cutting off the ear of the high priest's servant. He was at once rebuked by Jesus, and in the account by Luke, the doctor, we read that Jesus reached out and touched the man's head and healed him.

Jesus was perfectly in control of events. He was the one who was calm and at peace. This alone must have unnerved the others in the garden, including Judas. Or could it have been that Judas was sure Jesus would have called the angels to his aid, shown his power, demonstrated dramatically who he was? Perhaps Judas was waiting to see that happen before aligning himself again as one of the friends. Jesus did demonstrate who he was, but not in the way expected, and Judas, the traitor, must have realized to his horror that he had betrayed the person who was the best friend he ever had. He had thrown away everything for thirty pieces of silver. It had all gone horribly wrong. It is recorded in one of the other Gospel accounts (Matt. 27:3-10) that Judas took back the money to the chief priests and said, "I have sinned by betraying innocent blood," but there was no comfort for Judas. No one cared; he was rejected; no one wanted to know him. And so, absolutely distraught and convicted of his sin, he went and did what, sadly, many people in their extremity do—he killed himself.

If only he had realized before he had changed sides what he was doing! If only he had grasped what Jesus had been telling him right up to the last moment! If only . . . if only. . . .

In a story set at the end of time, Jesus sits with eleven of his friends at the table. The meal is ready, but everyone seems to be waiting for someone to join them. Then there is a knock at the door, and Judas comes in and stands before Jesus with downcast eyes. "Come in, my friend," says Jesus. "We were waiting for you." Yes, I know that story is an imaginary one—and yet, knowing Jesus, knowing his love, could it not be true?

There is a streak of Judas in us all. We want things our way, and, when they don't go our way, we try to manipulate things and people. We push them to the limit, and sometimes tragically, as for Judas, everything goes wrong. We too crash headlong, and there seems no hope, no help, no way back. I remember singing an old gospel song years ago. It has always stuck in my mind, for its message is one of hope even in seeming hopelessness:

> There's a way back to God from the dark paths of sin;
> There's a door that is open and you may go in:
> At Calvary's cross is where you begin,
> When you come as a sinner to Jesus.
> —attributed to E. H. Swinstead

There is a way back for all of us, and the "if onlys" can be wiped away if we are willing to come in penitence for the past, come to Jesus and allow him to lift us up and bring us back into the circle of his friends.

Judas is a figure to take heed of. He reminds us that even one who had been so close to Jesus could turn away, could be an instrument of destruction. *What sort of a man could do that?* we ask ourselves in horror. The answer is someone like you and me. We need to recognize our own weakness, willfulness, and blindness. But at the same time we must take courage; there is a way back, as long as we are willing to take it. The door is open; we have to go through and accept the love and the forgiveness that await us. Sadly Judas went to the wrong place with his confession and remorse. If only he had gone to Jesus, things would have been so different for him.

Yes, you and I have a lot to learn from the life of Judas—and when the danger signals flash in our lives, let's make sure we stop and listen.

Chapter 16

What would you have done?

John 18:12-27

WE ALL JUMP to conclusions—very quickly—and often hold on to those snap conclusions permanently. We sum people up in a moment and we are bound to our decisions, without ever asking whether we really did have all the facts. Many a person has been damaged for life by an opinion expressed publicly by someone who jumped in without knowing anything of the background. Some of the more popular daily newspapers have much to answer for in the way they sloganize people in the news. The headlines overemphasize the seemingly obvious, and once someone has been headline news it is difficult to escape from that picture implanted in the minds of those who read the headlines and, without thinking, accepted them as true.

What about Peter? How do you think of him? Peter the impetuous, Peter the coward, Peter the boss. I tried a small experiment some time ago and asked a number of people at random what they knew about Peter. Without exception they mentioned first of all, "He denied Jesus three times"—that is, of course, those who knew anything at all about him! So maybe we could all do with taking another look at Peter before we also brand him as a coward and a person of no "stickability."

We are told that Peter and another disciple followed Jesus when he was arrested; they wanted to see where Jesus was being taken and what was going to happen. Rather than running away, they kept close, as close as they could. What would you have done? I fear I would have run as fast as my legs would have carried me away from the trouble, thankful to escape, wanting only the safety of home and the opportunity to think about my next move. Not Peter and his companion—they were prepared to stick close by Jesus. Could it be that they hoped to "spring" him or find out if there was any chance of a rescue mission?

The friend who was with Peter is unnamed. Tradition has it, and it would seem very well attested, that it was John, not naming himself out of a genuine humility and not wanting to boast that he stuck by Jesus when others had fled. It seems that John was able to gain admittance to the high priest's house because he was known. Perhaps he had delivered fish there in the past—his father's business was fish, and so the family would be no strangers to the household of the high priest. Whether that can be proved one hundred percent I am not sure, but it is a likely explanation for his being known and allowed in and being able to bring Peter in also.

The two men put themselves in a very dangerous position indeed, for they were in enemy territory. The servant girl who let them in looked at Peter and seemed to remember she had seen him before—hadn't she seen him around with Jesus? So she asked him, probably not in an accusing way but a merely curious way. "You are not also one of this man's disciples, are you?"

For the first time Peter was challenged about his relationship with Jesus. "I am not!" he said. He denied that he belonged to the company of the friends of Jesus.

Before you judge him harshly, think again—what would you have done? Changed your mind about going in perhaps? Peter walked even closer to danger. He stood by the fire with the servants of the high priest, with the soldiers on guard duty. The firelight would show him up even more clearly, and yet he stood there. But soon he was challenged again, this time by a number of them. Again Peter was adamant and again denied he was one of the disciples.

But then someone who had been in the garden of Gethsemane, a relative of the man whom Peter had struck with his sword, looked at him closely and asked, "Did I not see you in the garden with him?" Here was real trouble, for Peter could have been arrested for attacking another person, regardless of whose company he kept.

"No," insisted Peter; by now he must have been petrified. And at that precise moment a cock crowed. Whether it was an actual cock crowing or the 3:00 A.M. bugle call that was known as "cock-crow" doesn't really matter. Peter knew then that what Jesus had told him would happen, had happened. He would relive that moment many times.

What is the evidence against Peter? He did deny his Master three times; that is clear. What we need to ask ourselves is, *Why?* Was it pure cowardice? Was he frightened to death, afraid for his own skin? Maybe he was. Or could it be that, like many a person in a resistance movement or secret army, he was playing a part so as to remain at liberty, to be free to act on his Master's behalf if he had a chance? Here he was, as near as he possibly could be to Jesus—and where was his sword, the one he had used to cut off the servant's ear? Could it have been under his garment, ready to be used again should he be needed to come to his Master's aid?

You may come to the conclusion that Peter was a coward, that he was all bluff, and that when it came to the test he failed miserably. You could point to the stories of many heroic Christian martyrs who went to their death because they would not deny they belonged to Jesus. You could tell me of those who languish in prison today because they have bravely been willing to "stand up and be counted." All this is true. But before you brand Peter a coward as he stood by that fire surrounded by danger, remember what Peter became later. Consider too: Did his experience of failure make him a better man? Did it bring him into a closer relationship with Jesus? Did it enable him to be a more effective leader? Did it enable him to die a martyr's death with triumph? I believe the answer to all these questions is yes.

Perhaps we only get to know ourselves as we are when we are complete and utter failures—when we come to the end of ourselves, of our own abilities, or our own strength, of our own pride, and we are proved wrong. When we come to that point, and we realize to our horror and our shame just what we really are, then we can begin to grow up, to be of use to our Lord and Master.

I find failure hard to cope with, particularly my own. I like to "win 'em all." My own personal makeup is of a fighter who has the confidence (often very misplaced!) that I can cope on my own, can succeed where others have failed. I hold to the philosophy that "it will be all right in the end." There are times when I cry bitterly because I am a complete and utter failure. I fail my Lord, my loved ones, and my friends. I fail myself—and that is the hardest thing in the world to admit and come to terms with. In one way, I never come to terms with defeat and failure, but I can look at Peter and thank God for him. Thank God that he allowed his story to be recorded, "warts and all."

Peter hit the very bottom; he also hit the heights! The bottom is not a pleasant thing to hit—it hurts! I take heart from some words of Paul's. There was a man who rejoiced in his own strength and power! Yet he could say this about the tough times, about the weakness he had to endure and experience:

> Three times I appealed to the Lord about this, that it would leave me, but he said to me, "My grace is sufficient for you, for power is made perfect in weakness." So, I will boast all the more gladly of my weaknesses, so that the power of Christ may dwell in me. (2 Cor. 12:8-9)

While Peter was experiencing weakness, another man was gloating over his own strength. That man was Annas, a very nasty piece of work altogether. He was the former high priest, father-in-law of the one in office, Caiaphas, but still holding the reins and still using that office to feather his own nest. Annas was a man who had made his money from temple business, exploiting the pilgrims. He hated Jesus, for Jesus had shown him up when he had cleared out Annas's rotten business from the house of God. Jesus was bad news for Annas—but not for much longer. Now Annas had Jesus. He called the tune.

Annas had his moment of triumph—or so he thought. He tried to look in command, blusteringly impressive, and yet Jesus simply and calmly put the ball right back in his court: "I have spoken openly to the world. . . . I have said nothing in secret."

Annas could not deny this fact. Jesus had a public ministry. He wasn't going to say anything different now from what he had always said. As he stood before Annas, he was the one who stood in judgment in his holiness and integrity. He stood as a challenge. Annas stood before Jesus as a cheat, one who had defamed his calling. He would be known forever as such. He was an absolute failure as a man and as a priest, but the tragedy was that he didn't recognize that fact. He thought he was the tops, when he was actually the rock bottom.

We do well to look at Annas's life and then at our own, especially those of us who are marked as having the authority of God as ministers and as those in leadership positions. How do we use our authority? Is it for God or for our own advancement and to enhance our personal image?

It is so easy to pass judgment on others, on those we consider failures. How are we judged by the one we profess to serve? What will be the verdict passed on us by him? It is his verdict that matters, for that verdict decides our ultimate destiny.

Chapter 17

"He suffered under Pontius Pilate"

John 18:28–19:16

I WAS BROUGHT UP in a church school in the days when religious instruction was seen as of primary importance and "learning by heart" was the main teaching method used. At the time, it seemed a bit—or a lot—of a bore, learning collects and huge chunks of the Bible, reciting psalms and singing hymns. Now I thank God for that grounding in the Christian faith. It didn't make me a Christian, but it did enable me to acquire a mine of information in which to delve to discover what the faith was all about. And when I did come to a personal knowledge of Jesus Christ, the knowledge stored up in my mind was gloriously translated and became real for me.

Yet some of the things I learned by heart all those years ago were a problem to me at the time, not least because some words to a child can sound very much like another, with a totally different meaning. We may laugh at "Harold be thy name," but to a child the name "Harold" makes sense, where "hallowed" is quite beyond them. One of the names that confused me for several years was Pontius Pilate. We solemnly recited the creed at school, and I obediently said with all the others, ". . . suffered under Pontius Pirate." You can imagine the picture in my mind: to me he was a cross between Long John Silver and Errol Flynn—as I said, it was a long time ago, and I was a very avid movie-goer!

Pontius Pilate was the Roman governor—and more of a pirate than a diplomat. He had no sympathy for or understanding of the Jews and rubbed them the wrong way time after time. He never sought to make friends of them. I suppose he despised them. They were not worth anything to him except to be used in the interests of Rome and to make his own life easy. He did not want trouble, so any sign of it was firmly and brutally squashed. He also had a way of "putting his foot in" through tactless actions.

This was no way to govern; Pilate had been a bad choice, complaints had been brought against him with the Emperor Tiberius. The emperor was not pleased and did not want to be involved with the stupid mistakes of a governor, so Pilate was warned to keep the peace—or else! His position, like that of many who have served as government ministers, was shaky to say the least. It was not in his interests for complaints against him to come to the emperor's ears again. He knew that playing along with the Jews would best serve his own purposes, even though he had no time for them and did not understand their religious history, traditions, and culture.

When Jesus was brought to him for sentencing, Pilate must have groaned, "More trouble!" It was just what he wanted to avoid, but the Jewish authorities were determined that he should make the decision to send Jesus to his death. In the words of today, they "made the bullets for him to fire." Pilate wanted the Jews to make the decision. They retorted that they were not allowed to make such a decision; only the governor could do that, which was true. So Pilate began to play a game with the Jews—verbal chess, you could describe it, with Jesus as the pawn.

Pilate talked with Jesus, questioned him, hoping that Jesus would condemn himself. But he found that Jesus was challenging him in a totally new way. Pilate was beginning to realize that Jesus was no ordinary prisoner, no mere political upstart but someone who, though innocent of the charges brought against him, was a threat to him by his very innocence. Jesus claimed to speak the truth, but the world-weary Pilate, so used to deceiving and being deceived, had no place in his life for truth. "What is truth?" Pilate asked the question disparagingly. The answer stood before him—the one who was "the way, the truth, and the life." Perhaps there was something in Pilate—behind his defenses, his seeming self-sufficiency—that craved for truth, for something that made sense of life. Was it as he spoke those words "What is truth?" that he sensed the answer lay in the prisoner before him? He may not have understood the Jews; their religion was of no interest to him; he had no time for such things; he was the emperor's man. And yet—?

William Barclay, in his commentary on John's Gospel (Westminster Press, 1975), says this:

> It was not in cynical humour that Pilate asked this question; nor was it the question of a man who did not care. Here was the chink in [Pilate's] armour. He asked the question wistfully and wearily.
>
> Pilate by this world's standards was a successful man. He had come almost to the top of the Roman civil service; he was governor-general of a Roman province; but there was something missing. Here in the presence of this simple, disturbing, hated Galilaean, Pilate felt that for him the truth was still a mystery—and that now he had got himself into a situation where there was no chance to learn it. It may be [Pilate] jested, but it was the jest of despair.

Pilate still had the chance to be somebody—a real man. He was face-to-face with Jesus. He could have held out his hand, could have discovered for himself the truth, God's truth. He could have had a new life, could have found the peace he longed for. But there was a price to pay; he had to surrender to the one who was his prisoner. Trying to play for time, he told the waiting crowd that he could find no reason to condemn Jesus, and as the custom was to set free a prisoner at Passover time, would they accept "the King of the Jews"? In his own mind Pilate knew that Jesus was a king. There was no escape for Pilate that way. The crowd was out for blood, the blood of Jesus. The people screamed their demands even louder. "Not this man, but Barabbas!" For Barabbas they chose life—but Jesus must die.

Pilate bowed to their request and released Barabbas, then turned his attention again to Jesus. What was he to do with him?

The crowd wanted blood—they would have it! Maybe if they saw a bleeding and battered Jesus, they would be satisfied and not go on to demand the ultimate bloodletting. Maybe they would be content to see him bloodied and humiliated. So Pilate handed Jesus over to the soldiers for punishment in the barbaric manner meted out to those who upset the well-oiled wheels of government. Jesus was a nuisance, whether he was innocent or not. He had proved an embarrassment; he needed to be taught a lesson. Maybe it would deter other would-be kings.

The treatment meted out to Jesus was in no way unique. It happened then and it happens today, to many innocent men and women caught up in political tension, civil unrest, the clash between people of different colors and ideologies. The authorities think they have let them off lightly if they "give them a good hiding" and release them—at least they are alive. Some are not so fortunate; their bodies are found mutilated and battered, often miles away from the point of arrest. Many others are never seen again after the arrest—innocent men and women who have been unfortunate enough to be caught up in the power struggles of others. And we do not have to look as far as Chile or South Africa; it happens much nearer home.

So Jesus experienced what many a political prisoner experiences today—the beating, the horseplay of the brutal soldiers who find their entertainment in humiliating a fellow human being, putting him through the farce of a mock homage.

Their job done, the soldiers took Jesus back to Pilate. What does Pilate think as he views Jesus? Do his words spoken earlier to the prisoner, "What is truth?" stick in his throat and heart? Is he ashamed of the depths to which he and his fellow Romans have sunk? Does he feel pity for Jesus? At any rate he goes out to the Jewish crowd waiting for the verdict and again tells the people he has no reason to condemn Jesus; there is no case to answer. Then he brings Jesus to them. "Here is the man!" The translation of the words he used is more like "Look at this poor fellow." You would have thought the sight of Jesus, of any man, in that state would have brought the crowd to their senses. You could have hoped for pity, a feeling of guilt, a turning away in shame. But no, like a pack of wolves with the scent of blood in their nostrils, the people are eager for the final destruction. "Crucify him! Crucify him!" is their hysterical response to the sight of Jesus.

Pilate stands his ground and again tells them he has no reason to find Jesus guilty; there is no evidence. "We have a law, and according to that law he ought to die because he has claimed to be the Son of God," insists the crowd. Pilate is scared stiff; he realizes he is out of his depth, he cannot cope with the situation. Jesus frightens him more than the crowd. Pilate can cope with hatred; he has seen it all before. He cannot cope with goodness, with innocence, with the truth, for if Jesus is the Son of God . . . ?

Now even the prisoner remains silent before him. There are no words of explanation, no plea for mercy; Jesus says nothing. But he does not need to speak. Pilate knows in his heart that this man should not die. He pleads with Jesus to answer, reminding Jesus that he has the power of life and death over him by virtue of his office as governor. But Jesus' reply sends shivers down Pilate's spine, for Jesus reminds him that Pilate has power only because God has given it to him—what an awesome responsibility!

Pilate knows clearly what he should do, so he tries to reason with the crowd. But the people, realizing his weakness, play their trump card: "If you release this man, you are no friend of the emperor." It is blackmail now, and Pilate knows it. They have hit him where it hurts. He knows that his own career, his own life are finished unless he goes against his better judgment. And so he gives in to the mob.

Pilate knows that Jesus is king, for he has proved it without a doubt, and yet he has to die. "Here is your King!" says Pilate, but there is no shout of acclamation, no trumpet sounds, no royal salute—only the insistent shouts of "Crucify him!" Pilate, in mocking tone, asks the question to which he already has the answer. "Shall I crucify your King?" But the chief priests, gleefully knowing they have won the day, negate the fundamental heart of their faith: "We have no king but the emperor." They deny their God whom they claim to worship. They have won the day, but they have lost everything. They have bowed to Rome; they have betrayed their prophets, priests, and kings, and God. The priests of the chosen people have chosen to go the way of the world; they have deposed the everlasting God for an earthly pagan despot in acknowledging the emperor as their king.

Professor Leon Morris, in *The Gospel According to John*, says this of the chief priests: "They spoke in terms of cynical expediency. But they expressed the real truth." They had no king but the dictate of a foreign power; they had sunk to that point, by choice. They had turned their back on God's gift; soon they would see him nailed down and launched up into the sky for all to see. What sort of a king was that? For them, even a foreign heathen power was to be preferred! And Pilate? He had done his best in a way; he had tried to save Jesus; he had done more than many another would have done. But pride and fear won the day; his job and his skin mattered most.

The events of that day are reenacted over and over again. The names, the places, and the dates are different, but the story is the same. There are those who "dot the i's and cross the t's," who make sure they observe the religious niceties, play their part in ceremonials, do not defile their bodies by entering into forbidden territory and yet blaspheme and pollute by their greed and anger, their pettiness, their craving for power. There are those who know what they should be, what they should do; they halfheartedly point in the right direction but waver; they are afraid to do wrong but afraid to do right. What finally decides them is not truth but expediency. They take the easy way out. They cannot pay the price of truth.

Pilate could have saved Jesus. He had the power, but he wasn't prepared to use it to save him, wasn't prepared to face the consequences from "on high." There are many Pilates today who sit in the seats of power, who are called to make judgments and pass sentence, and they do so influenced by public demand, political pressure, personal preference, and their own pride and fears. Look around the world—there they sit, there they pontificate—and watch how they fall!

There's a bit of Pilate in me. I do my best, make my points, but then when things get nasty I draw back. And there are times when, out of fear of what people will think of me or pride in what I think I am, I capitulate. I know, of course, in my heart of hearts when I have taken the coward's way out and let selfishness and pride win the day. Sometimes I am able to redress the balance, to confess or apologize, but sadly, most times I just let it go and hope no one will remember.

Did Pilate think anyone would remember what happened that day? After all, it was just one event among many. Just another poor wretch who opened his mouth too much, who didn't watch his manners, got on the wrong side of the powers that be, and who was made a public example. Men on crosses were a dime a dozen in his day; life had always been cheap. Who would remember Jesus of Nazareth, the wandering preacher, the chap who worked miracles, who ruffled the feathers of the local religious leaders? Who would remember him, his life or his death, and the people who were part of both? It would all die down in time. It always did—didn't it?

Poor Pilate, forever to be known as the one who sent Jesus to his death, who turned him over for execution! He did not know that two thousand years later people would still speak his name as they stood to affirm the Lordship of Jesus Christ—the King who "suffered under Pontius Pilate, was crucified, died, and was buried . . . ." It is easy to be wise after the event, isn't it?

Will anyone remember my cowardice, my sitting on the fence, my misplaced pride? I have the awful feeling and the chilling assurance within me that someone will, unless I do something about it—now.

Chapter 18

He is the King

John 19:17-24

PILATE HAD TRIED to save Jesus. He had done his best, but his best had not been good enough. The chief priests, with their theological arguments and their veiled threats, and the crowd, getting larger and nastier by the minute, had finally won; Pilate handed Jesus over to them. It was just a matter of time before Jesus would be nailed to the cross, for there would be no last-minute change of heart or reprieve.

Now the routine of execution begins, with the condemned man carrying his own execution block. Could human beings stoop so low as to make a man carry the instrument of his own death? But there is nothing new under the sun. How often we read of men and women being made to dig their own graves before being killed, adding yet another cruel twist to the occasion, another sadistic turn of the screw to the cold, calculating cruelty of humankind.

So Jesus staggers along, battered and bleeding, with the cross on his back, going the way many a man had gone before him, and many a man after. Mark's Gospel records that a passerby was compelled to carry Jesus' cross for him, but Jesus was made to carry it himself for most of the way at any rate. In the jeering, howling crowd that lined the route, were there any who, as Pilate had done, pointed to Jesus and said, "Look at the poor fellow"? I feel sure there would have been—maybe among those who had been healed or helped by Jesus, who had known the touch of his hand, his words of comfort and assurance in their pain and despair. Those who had felt that Jesus was their hope and their future now saw the sorry spectacle of him in defeat, a prisoner on his way to death.

Perhaps too there were those who knew nothing of him but who felt sorry for "the poor fellow" and turned away shuddering to think of the pain he would have to endure before death finally brought him release.

Pilate may have lost his battle for the life of Jesus, but he had one last card he could and did play. A sign was customarily prepared to declare the name and the crime of each person to be executed. This would be publicly displayed as the prisoner made his way to the place of execution, so that all would see who he was and what crime he had committed. It could act as a useful deterrent, an awful warning to any who may have felt inclined to commit another such offense. Finally it would be fixed on the cross as a macabre headboard. Pilate wrote the inscription for Jesus; it was his chance to say the last word on Jesus, and so he wrote, "Jesus of Nazareth, the King of the Jews." To make sure everyone could read and understand it, he deliberately wrote it in the three great languages commonly in use: Hebrew, Latin, and Greek.

The chief priests were furious. They demanded that Pilate amend it to read, "This man *said*, 'I am King of the Jews'" [italics added]. Pilate refused to alter what he had written; at last he dug his heels in. He had been beaten by the Jews in the battle over Jesus when they used their trump card against him by declaring their allegiance to Rome. So let them taste the power of Rome. Pilate declared his judgment on Jesus and let the world see it: "What I have written I have written."

You could say that what Pilate did was "too little, too late." Maybe he did it out of annoyance, determined to rub the noses of the priests in the dirt they had descended to; he wanted to humiliate them as they had humiliated him. I would like to think that Pilate also did it for Jesus, because Jesus had convinced him of his right to the title. Yes, maybe it was "too little, too late," but it was better than nothing; it was an acknowledgment of the truth.

Too little, too late! Do you ever feel as I do, that the little we could do is not worth doing because it is too late? What use is an afterthought, a post-event protest? Those occasions when we lack the guts to do anything about a situation until the opportunity has passed and time has run out—what is the use of protesting then, after it has happened? I don't believe action is ever wasted. We may have to eat humble pie ourselves, because our very protesting after the event shows us up as cowards, people who did not have the courage of their own convictions at the time it really mattered. Yet we should respond to the voice of conscience and do the little we can, even in retrospect—for who knows what it may accomplish?

Pilate's weakness was recorded for all time, but so was his protest, his stand for Jesus. So I take heart from that; it shows that the belated token stand—yes, even yours and mine—can be used to bring glory to God, and knowing that should encourage us even when all seems lost through our own weakness.

That sign on the cross must have infuriated the Jews. There it was for all to see and read and ponder on. It was the verdict of Rome on Jesus of Nazareth. It still stands for all the world to see, to read, and to ponder on.

For the soldiers who carried out the execution, it would make little difference who the man on the cross was. He was just another job, all part of a day's work; they were the ones on duty at the time, so they carried out the execution. They were not personally involved. They didn't understand the issue. They were only concerned to get the assignment over and divide the spoils among themselves, the belongings of the executed man that were the perks of their trade. They were quite indifferent to the sufferings, only concerned for their share of what was to be had. So there they were, playing a game as Jesus died. Callous, brutal, hard men, professional soldiers, just doing their duty, obeying orders; feelings did not enter into it.

The other Gospel accounts record that the officer on duty was affected. He must have attended many crucifixions as duty officer, but he saw something different in this man's going to his death. He was convinced of his innocence. And more than that, he was sure that Jesus was a good man; could it even be possible that this man was the Son of God? He watched him die and came to his conclusion and voiced it.

The Roman officer looked and saw who Jesus really was; he recognized God on the cross. Jesus would not have looked like a god hanging there; he would have looked "a poor fellow." But the Roman saw what others missed, saw the divine clothed in battered, bleeding, dying human flesh.

In the chapel of the Trinity and All Saints College in Horsforth in Leeds there is a crucifix. It dominates that chapel, and as soon as you enter, your eyes are drawn to it. I have seen it many times, and each time it speaks to me afresh of Jesus who suffered and died for me, who gave his life in its prime for me. It makes me want to weep, for I realize that it is my sin that put Jesus on the cross, just as much as if I had personally hammered in the nails. But it also speaks to me of the voluntary nature of the suffering. Jesus died because he loved men and women so much—men and women of all generations, including me. For it was love that held him there, not the nails of humans.

In 1986, Yorkshire Television recorded a service in that chapel. The service was specially for people who suffered from communication disorders, their families and friends, and those who cared for them. As the Anglican Adviser to Yorkshire Television, I spent a great deal of time in the chapel as preparations were made and rehearsals went on, and so I was able to look at that particular cross from many angles. I found that time a very moving experience, particularly in the context of the service we were recording.

The preacher at the service was Canon Jim Richardson, then Vicar of Leeds, and he too, in his sermon, pointed to that cross, saying with reference to suffering and pain:

> Isn't that the message of this chapel crucifix? The suffering
> Christ who in his own body reveals to us the true nature of
> God. Not remote and unreal, but Love itself. But note the
> rebellion too. The body is arched away from the cross. It is
> straining upwards. The sigh for humanity is there, but it
> anticipates the resurrection, and the victory over sin, evil, and
> death in all their forms. Christ reigns on that tree!

Yes—"King of kings and Lord of lords . . . He shall reign for ever and ever." But there are still those who are indifferent, those who reject him, those who hate him. There are still those who play games and ignore him. That is their choice. There are also those who look and see and begin to understand what he is all about and who go on to discover for themselves the glorious truth written in flesh on the tree.

Jesus was lifted up, as he said he would be. He drew and still draws men and women to meet him, to follow him. But beware before you make your decision, for he said this: "If any want to become my followers, let them deny themselves and take up their cross daily and follow me" (Luke 9:23).

Look at the cross—that is the price of love. If you follow the one who died on the cross, it could cost you your life too. Think carefully, very carefully, before you decide.

Chapter 19

Love is stronger than death

John 19:25-37

IT WAS NO PLACE for them to be, watching an execution, particularly one like this. For death was not to come swiftly—with the flash of a blade, the violent pull on the end of a rope, or the sickening thud of a club—but as the result of a slow, agonizing, barbaric form of torture. The atmosphere was horrendous for anyone with an ounce of feeling in them. Think of that scene—three men's being executed publicly, the crowd's seeing it as frightening entertainment, some jeering and shouting in triumph, gloating over those who had caused them trouble, and who now would trouble them no more. The soldiers, in their rough, callous way, kept order and made sure that everything went according to plan with military precision. Think too of the heat, the flies, the noise, the dust, and the smell.

It was no place for anyone who cared for any of those poor wretches being executed. Certainly no place for a woman! Much better if women were kept well away. It was bad enough to know what was happening, but actually seeing it—it could turn their minds. They could always visit the grave afterward, take some flowers, have someone around to comfort them in the peace and quiet, but to be at the actual execution—no.

It was no place for them to be but the only place they could be; it was the place of love. What a sad little group! There was Jesus' mother, Mary, and her sister; Mary, the wife of Clopas (one ancient tradition says that Clopas was the brother of Joseph, so that would make her the sister-in-law of Mary, Jesus' mother); and the fourth woman, Mary Magdalene, who had once been healed by Jesus. With the quartet of sorrowing women was John, the one disciple brave enough to come so close to the scene. John bore a double burden, his own deep sorrow and the task of comforting and supporting those weeping women. It says a lot about John to know that he was there, that he was the one who stood by the women as well as by Jesus. He must have been a tremendous support during their dreadful ordeal.

How did Jesus feel as he looked down from the cross on that little group of people who loved him so much that they were willing to undergo the agony of being there, unable to do anything but stand by him and love him with all their hearts? Jesus saw his heartbroken mother and he saw his friend. He said to his mother, of John, "Here is your son"; and to John, as he entrusted his mother to him, "Here is your mother." He brought them into a special relationship with each other, so that they could comfort and care for one another; they would be good for one another in the days that lay ahead.

Jesus knew the importance of human relationships. He fully understood loneliness, "being left." On the cross he experienced terrible loneliness; he felt forsaken, even by his Father. He knew what loneliness was like. He went through it.

Perhaps the greatest burden of bereavement for anyone is that of "being left"—feeling totally alone, with no one to share things with, no one to care deeply about him or her. As I have been writing this, I have been talking to a man who has, in the space of a few months, lost his wife, his son, and his daughter-in-law. "I live on my own," he told me. "It's awful. I keep picking up things that belonged to them, and they've gone, and I'm all on my own, and nobody knows what it's like."

Nobody knows what it's like—except someone who has gone through it. And Jesus has gone through it. He does know. He does care. The song "Eleanor Rigby" includes the words "All the lonely people, where do they all come from?" So many lonely people— especially those who have been bereaved, who have lost the one who meant everything to them, and life now seems empty and hollow.

Jesus brought together two desperately lonely and sad people, his mother and John. I believe he wants to bring the lonely and sad together today. I look around the church and see the folk who live alone, who sit alone, who are alone. They need someone, they need one another. Perhaps we should remember what Jesus did when he introduced John and his mother into a new and special relationship. They both knew and loved him; he was their common bond. So why are there so many lonely and isolated Christians? Perhaps you are one. Could it be that Jesus is asking you to be a mother, a son, or a special friend to someone in the same position? Would you be brave enough, caring enough, to make the first move—for his sake?

Jesus knew that his mother would be well cared for. He knew now that his friend had a mother to love and be loved by. As a son and as a friend, he had lovingly cared for them to the end. He had looked to their future and made provision for them. What an example of love! In all his desperate suffering, he was concerned for those he loved and who loved him.

When I am in pain, worried, or fearful, my thoughts are entirely self-centered. I can only see me and my troubles. I want the world to revolve around me. When I am hurt by someone else, my only concern is for myself. I cannot see further than Margaret Cundiff. Yet I read of the care Jesus took of others when he was hanging from the cross, when he was suffering so terribly because of the hatred and rottenness of those who had put him there. He was still concerned, still loving, still planning for the good of other people. It makes me hang my head in shame at my own selfishness and lack of love and concern, at the "I" that is so uppermost in my mind that it often obliterates the crying needs of others.

Jesus suffered—really suffered—in every part of himself. How thirsty he must have been. How much he longed for just a taste of something cool on his parched lips. His cry "I am thirsty" was met with a wet sponge full of cheap wine, raised to his lips in a last act of kindness. Maybe one of the soldiers felt sorry for him and in a rough-and-ready manner did what he could for "that poor fellow." The one who did that act is unknown to us but known to Jesus, appreciated forever. It was just a small act. Probably the one who did it never gave it another thought and would have been astonished to know that his act would be remembered two thousand years later, will be remembered as long as time lasts. "Little things mean a lot," says the old song. Yes they do, and we are all capable of little acts of kindness, the response to need, "putting ourselves out."

I was hurrying along the road one afternoon, intent on getting to the bank before it closed, when an old lady touched my arm and said, "Are you going across the road?" "No," I replied and was about to rush on when she said very wistfully, "Only I can't see very well and I'm frightened of the traffic." I must admit that part of me still wanted to rush on, but I turned around, got hold of her arm and slowly we walked to the crossing, waited, and went across. As we made it to the other side, she turned and smiled at me. "God bless you, luv," she said. I felt a real heel!

My response of caring had not been immediate or spontaneous, but I was so glad she gave me a second chance to do what I knew I should—and the bank was still open when I got there! Cheap wine on a sponge meant so much to Jesus. Our small, simple acts of kindness mean so much to those around who are in need of maybe just a hand, a smile, a lift, a word.

Jesus received that gift of a drink, then he "bowed his head and gave up his spirit." Luke records that he said, "Father, into your hands I commend my spirit" (Luke 23:46). It was the prayer every Jewish child said on going to bed. Jesus died like a child going to sleep, secure in the love of his Father, with perfect trust and confidence as he fell asleep. What better words to be on our lips as we put our head on the pillow each night? What better words to be on our lips and in our heart as we close our eyes, even for the last time?

Jesus was dead, but the soldier made doubly sure by plunging his spear into his side. Jesus was dead all right—very dead. The other two men who had been crucified may have shown some signs of being still alive, so their legs were smashed to finish them off. Time was now short before the Sabbath day, and as the Sabbath day was holy, the Jews did not want bodies hanging about. Get rid of them, get them out of the way, forget what had happened; the Sabbath must not be disturbed.

"Out of sight, out of mind." The crowd would disperse, to go home and get ready for the Sabbath. The soldiers would tidy up and report back to barracks, then go off to enjoy themselves with their families, meeting their girlfriends, getting drunk, sleeping it off—whatever soldiers find to do when they have finished their duties. Already the hours on duty would be receding from their memories, and tomorrow was another day.

Yes, life goes on, even after a death, even after many deaths. Time goes relentlessly on: the minutes, the hours, the days, the years. "Time, like an ever-rolling stream, Bears all its sons away." It was just another crucifixion day, just another three men thrust into eternity, a very ordinary day really, just like any other. Those who lived through that day would not know it would forever have a special name—"Good Friday." "Good" Friday? Not much good about it, was there? It was a bleak, bad, horrible day. For some it was the worst day of their lives; for others, a day of revenge and satisfaction, a day that had brought the worst out in them. But it was "Good Friday" for all who would look to the one who hung on the cross— the man in the middle—and put their trust in him.

> He died that we might be forgiven;
> He died to make us good,
> That we might go at last to heaven,
> Saved by his precious blood.
> —C. F. Alexander (1818–95)

He did that on Good Friday; he did it for you and for me. What effect has it on us? We know the story well, but how real is it for us now?

At our Family Service at Easter time, a group of our church

members were portraying the death of Jesus in pantomime. A young man, Jonathan, was playing the part of Jesus. Blows were aimed at him as he was hoisted roughly onto a platform at the front of the church. His arms were stretched out, the make-believe nails hammered in. It was a most moving portrayal of the crucifixion; we were all deeply impressed by it. But of course, we knew the story; we knew what was happening.

From my seat I could see not only the drama but the rapt expressions on the faces of the congregation, and I thought, "We must do this more often; it really holds their attention." Then suddenly an agonized scream rang through the quiet church, followed by uncontrollable crying. It went through me, as I am sure it did through every person in the church. It came from a very small person, only a year old, who had been watching wide-eyed from the safety of a comfortable pair of knees. She was only a baby; she did not know the story; she was too young to understand. So why was she so distressed? Why was her pain so real? It was quite simple. Jonathan, who was playing the part of Jesus, was her daddy. All she knew was that Daddy was being hurt; she could do nothing to help him; she could not even get to him. She could only express her feelings in desperate crying and screaming. It took a long time before Rachel was pacified that morning, but later, cradled in her father's arms, she eventually allowed herself to be comforted and knew that everything was all right then.

Perhaps that morning all of us in the church learned something very important. We learned it not by our heads, intellectually accepting the suffering and death of Jesus, but through the crying of a child responding to her father's pain and through seeing the real anguish on that young father's face as he played out his part while his daughter cried. It was not just good acting; it was real, for he could do nothing to relieve his child's distress until his part had been played out.

The death of Jesus is so familiar that maybe we have lost something by its very familiarity. It took a child's scream and a young father's pained face to remind me of what "Good Friday" was really about. It brought me afresh to look at the cross and to look at myself and to re-echo the words written by Isaac Watts (1674–1748):

> Were the whole realm of nature mine,
> that were an offering far too small;
>   love so amazing, so divine,
> demands my soul, my life, my all.

Chapter 20 ⟿

Now he's dead and gone

John 19:38—20:10

W HEN IS THE FUNERAL?" That is one of the first questions
we ask when we receive news of the death of a relative or
friend. We want to show our respect and love by being there, sending flowers, getting in touch with the family. The funeral arrangements are made by the next of kin, the one closest to the person
who has died. The next of kin has to make all the arrangements with
the funeral director. There are friends to be contacted, usually the
bank and the insurance companies to be informed; there is so much
to be done within the space of a very short time. But there is often
another member of the family, a close friend, who will help with
all the running around and be an arm to lean on while the necessary but very emotional details have to be dealt with.

What would happen to Jesus' body? Would anyone be allowed
to have it? After all, Jesus had been put to death by the authorities;
it was up to them to decide about the disposal of the body—they
could do with it what they willed. It was likely that they would
want to oversee the arrangements, particularly since Jesus had made
some extravagant claims about rising from the dead. It could be that
his friends would fabricate a story about his coming back to life, so
the authorities would want a very close watch put on his body, certainly until all the interest in Jesus had died down.

Who was the next of kin? Surely it was Jesus' mother or one of
his brothers or even one of his close friends, one of those who had
been his companions during the last three years. Yet it was none
of them but Joseph of Arimathea who went to Pilate and asked for
the body. An interesting character was Joseph. He was rich and

influential, a member of the council called the Sanhedrin, which had tried Jesus. But Joseph had not agreed with either the way the council had gone about the trial or the decision the members had come to. Luke tells us, "Now there was a good and righteous man named Joseph, who . . . was waiting expectantly for the kingdom of God" (Luke 23:50-51).

Joseph had spoken out on behalf of Jesus but would not take a stand as one of his followers, for he was afraid of his fellow councilors. So he became a secret follower, not prepared to nail his colors to the mast and take the risk of losing his position, even though he believed Jesus was right.

Now Jesus was dead, so maybe it was as well that Joseph had not declared himself a follower; he could have lost everything and been left with nothing. Yet he boldly went and asked for the body, acting as "next of kin," you could say. He found the courage now that he had lacked before. How do you explain that?

He was joined by fellow member of the Sanhedrin Nicodemus, who provided all the spices for the anointing of Jesus' body and assisted Joseph with the preparation and the burial. Nicodemus was a fascinating character too. Early on in Jesus' ministry, Nicodemus had come at night to talk with him about spiritual issues; he wanted to find out the truth and was willing to listen to the wandering preacher. He wasn't too proud to ask, but he was too timid to ask publicly. The conversation between the two has been the means of countless persons' coming into faith. One of the best-loved verses in the Bible is "For God so loved the world that he gave his only Son, so that everyone who believes in him may not perish but may have eternal life" (John 3:16). It has been preached on and written about times without number. It has been set to music in every style from classic to pop and rock and has been the word of assurance to many a timid soul who has come wanting to know for sure that they could really have a new start.

Now Nicodemus saw the dead and battered body of Jesus and did what he could to afford him a dignified burial. Joseph and Nicodemus—two men who, if they had spoken out, if they had been brave, if they had been true to their convictions, might have saved Jesus. How did they feel as they saw his body, as they anointed him and wrapped him in the grave clothes? What did they say? What could they say?

We cannot stand in judgment on those two men unless we can put our hand on our heart and say we have never failed in our witness, never let an opportunity go by to share Jesus, never been at all reticent in going into "the lion's den." I look into my own heart and have to confess that I have failed to speak out; I have been too concerned for my own position, my own standing. I have been in gatherings where "simple faith" has been scorned, where those who claim to have been "converted" or "born again" have been regarded with amusement and as suspect candidates for any high office. And there have been times when I have kept quiet. Oh yes, I was content to scurry back home and be known there as a "born-again, converted, Bible-believing Christian"—but not in some sophisticated, high-powered centers of discussion and learning. I do not want to appear as "the country cousin," or "just a good simple woman"—not me! So I keep quiet or lamely make some half-hearted comment.

Joseph and Nicodemus were the bravest of the brave, heroes of the faith compared with me—and perhaps with you too! They were brave when all seemed lost. Or could it have been that those Jesus' last days, including his death, had finally convinced them, against all the odds, against all human reasoning, that this Jesus was the Son of God, in spite of his seeming defeat? As they tenderly and reverently laid his body to rest, was there within them the seed of hope that this was not the last they would see or hear of Jesus? As the stone was rolled against the entrance to the tomb, did they really think it was the end? What was in their minds as they left the scene? There was no doubt that the cross was already acting as a symbol of triumph rather than failure, for two silent men had now found their voices and their courage, the strength to act, the power to witness, but little did they know then what was to follow. All they knew was that they had done what they knew they had to do. And perhaps that is what we are called to do day by day—to do what we know we should do, and do it for him.

Sunday morning a sorrowing woman, Mary Magdalene, came to visit the grave. Brave woman! She had stood by the cross with that small, devoted, and devastated group of people, witnessing the terrible events, the desolation, the darkness of death. She loved Jesus so much. He had given her a new life; she would have given it gladly for him. Now he was dead and all she could do was pay her last respects. She must have been totally exhausted, both physically and mentally, yet she came in the darkness of the early morning to be near Jesus. So much for the argument about women's being the weaker sex, being unable to cope with the traumas and tragic events of life like men can! Women may be weaker physically, but because of their capacity to love so deeply and intently, they can and often do overcome seemingly impossible odds through that power of love, finding a strength beyond their own.

Mary came to the tomb—and what she saw when she arrived must almost have finished her. It was the final blow: The stone at the entrance had been removed; the body was gone. And so, shocked and distraught, she ran to tell Peter and John the dreadful news. It must have seemed to her the end of the world—her world. Surely nothing could be worse than what had happened now! There was no depth below this. It was the end.

There are times when we think we have reached the end of our tether and will snap altogether, times when there is no hope, no help. I remember a Sunday morning when Trevor, a Methodist minister, was preaching at one of the united services we hold from time to time in Selby. In the course of his sermon, Trevor said, "When you think you are at the end of your tether, remember who holds the other end." That morning Trevor made a new start, with a new confidence that has not left him or let him go.

Mary was at the end of her tether. My friend in church that morning was at the end of his. I've been at the end of mine many times, and no doubt so have you. But remember Jesus, the one who holds the other end, who will never let you go, who will hold you safe for all eternity—the one who was "crucified, died, and was buried" but who did not remain so. No tomb could hold him, no stone withhold him, no grave clothes restrain him, no human power defeat him—nor us either.

Chapter 21

But how do you know it was he?

John 20:11-18

SOME YEARS AGO a group from my parish went for an outing in the Yorkshire Dales. Everyone had walked steadily uphill, and finally we found ourselves on a grassy stretch of flat ground, an ideal stopping-place for our picnic lunch. We had settled down to enjoy lunch, sunbathe, and rest from our strenuous walk when we heard shouting and saw someone running toward us. We could not make out the words properly—the runner was almost hysterical—but we quickly realized that one of our party, the vicar's small son, had fallen over the edge of a sheer drop.

We all began to scramble to our feet. James, the vicar, followed by some of the men, raced in the direction of the cliff. We were absolutely terrified, sure that Philip was dead at the bottom of the cliff. But by a miracle he had been caught up in a bush, the only bush there was, and was rescued, scratched, crying but unhurt, his main complaint being that he had lost his sandal. He soon recovered from his ordeal, but for the rest of us it was a very frightening experience that took a long time to get over. There were many racing hearts that day, with blood pressures sky high. We shuddered to think what might have been; it was not an experience any of us would like to go through again.

As I read of Mary's dashing off with the news that the tomb is empty and Jesus' body gone, her incoherently spilling out the story to Peter and John who then run off toward the tomb, I see in my mind's eye the scene in the Dales. I sense the absolute fear and confusion, hear the thudding of men's feet and the heavy breathing, feel the perspiration rise—born of fear and exertion. Peter goes into the tomb and sees that it is as Mary has said—the tomb is empty. The neatly placed grave clothes are there, but the one who had been wrapped in them has gone. John quickly joins Peter and sees for himself. They both know Mary is telling the truth—it is no delusion. The tomb is wide open to the world; Jesus is definitely not there, but where is he? Peter and John return home, no doubt to share the grim news, to ask if anyone has heard anything that might throw some light, to try to make sense of all this.

And Mary? She remains outside the tomb, glued to the spot, crying. It is the end of her world. She is unable to move, frozen by grief. Then she takes a look inside the tomb—maybe the body has been moved around but is still there; perhaps there may be some clue as to what has happened. She sees two angels, dressed in white, sitting where Jesus had been lying. They ask her why she is crying, and she tells them, "They have taken away my Lord, and I do not know where they have laid him." She is not interested in the angels nor in awe of them; all she can think of is Jesus. She is asked a question and gives her answer.

How would you have reacted to the sight of two angels—or even one, for that matter? How did she know they were angels? All that John records is that they were angels. Were they two of the ones who sang with joy at Jesus' birth, I wonder. What is certain is that there is a good case for angels. Their existence is recorded for us in the Bible; they were accepted by those who wrote down the events that took place. So we can be sure that angels do exist.

There is someone else now at the tomb. He asks Mary the same question as the angels: "Why are you weeping?" And then he adds, "Whom are you looking for?" Mary realizes that here is someone who might help her to find Jesus. Maybe he is the one who has moved the body. Perhaps he works in the garden. So many ideas are going through her head. Now she has a chance to find out what has happened, and if this man is the one who removed the body, then perhaps he will tell her where it is, and she can go to get it back. Brave, loving Mary! What an example of commitment to Jesus! Nothing would hold her back from her Lord; she would stand against the world for him, resist the strongest and fiercest for him. She didn't know who "they" were, what she was up against, but she was determined to overcome anything and anyone to be reunited with Jesus. Then the man says one word, her name— "Mary."

She knows instantly he is no gardener. She recognizes his voice. There is no doubt who he is—he is Jesus.

This raises questions in some people's minds. Why was it that she didn't recognize him at first? Where was he when Peter and John came? And the biggest question of all, how could she be so sure it was Jesus? Could she have been mistaken, in such a state of shock, grief, and terror that her mind played tricks and she was having hallucinations? Mary was sure enough. And now she wants to hold him, grasp him, fling her arms around him, be held by him, but he stops her from doing so. He does not allow her to hang on and keep him to herself. He has work for her to do. She is to go and tell the others he is alive; he has risen from the dead as he promised.

So she goes, this time running with joy. This time it is good news, the greatest news, the seemingly impossible news, the news Jesus' friends didn't dare think about because it was beyond their wildest hopes and dreams—Jesus is alive! "I have seen the Lord," says Mary.

I hardly think that Jesus' friends would have believed Mary at first. The terrible time they had all gone through would mean they were in a complete daze, and Mary—well, she had suffered more than most. She'd seen everything, seen Jesus crucified, seen the empty tomb, seen . . . seen what . . . who? Had she really? Do you think she did meet with Jesus, or was she deluded? Was it all just wishful thinking translated into a human mirage?

I believe it was just as John's Gospel says it was. You may think this story is too good to be true, but surely it is too good not to be true! It rings true!

Once in London I was walking through Trafalgar Square. It was crowded with people, many of them tourists, chattering away in every language under the sun; businessmen and women were trying to push their way through, heading for the station; there was a roar and a rumble of traffic all around, and I heard a voice say, "Margaret!" I knew, although I could not see, who it was. There was no mistaking the voice. Not that it was any louder, higher, or deeper than any of the many voices around—but it was a voice I recognized, and I knew who it was by the way he spoke my name. It was an old friend whom I had not seen for a long time; certainly I had no idea he was in London that day. But I knew who it was before my eyes made him out, walking toward me smiling, his hand outstretched.

I expect you have had similar experiences. Someone has called your name, and although there may have been a hundred there with the same name, you knew it was for you because of the tone, the inflection in the voice—you just knew!

I am sure Mary got it right too! It was Jesus. He lovingly chose her to be the first person to meet him after his resurrection, and he called her by name. That gives me great heart! Whatever may be said for or against the ordination of women, however much discussion takes place on whether a woman is capable of being a minister, in the end it doesn't really matter. For I know there were women who stood by Jesus, even as he died; it was a woman who was the first to see him alive; it was to a woman that he gave the privilege of telling others. Whatever men or women or the church may think about the ministry of women, Jesus himself was a great supporter and encourager of women, giving them a ministry and mission in his name.

What really matters is not the argument about men or women or even angels but the fact that Jesus is alive. He is risen. He is alive forevermore.

He is still meeting with people as personally as he did that day when he spoke to Mary by name. He knows each one of us by name, and if you will listen you will hear him—even at this very moment.

Speak, Lord, in the stillness,
  While I wait on Thee;
Hushed my heart to listen
In expectancy.

. . . .

Fill me with the knowledge
  Of Thy glorious will;
All Thine own good pleasure
In Thy child fulfill.

—Emily M. Crawford (1868–1927)

Chapter 22

Behind closed doors

John 20:19-29

JUST DOWN THE ROAD from our home is Carlton Towers, the Yorkshire home of the Duke of Norfolk. Originally built in the seventeenth century, and much rebuilt in 1820 and 1874, it is surrounded by extensive grounds and is now open to the public at certain times of the year. While not as large or as well known as some of the other stately homes, it is attracting an increasing number of visitors, who enjoy exploring the grounds and seeing round the house, which is still very much lived in. One of the fascinating rooms upstairs houses a "priest's hole," and the guide explains to visitors that during the time when it was an offense punishable by law to take part in a Roman Catholic service or to harbor a Roman Catholic priest, this secret hideaway was used by priests visiting the house, where they could be safe from the officers of the Crown. When the premises were searched, there would be no sign of a priest or of a Mass being celebrated. Only when the officers had left, satisfied that no one illegal was in the house, would the signal be given and those behind the locked and secret door be able to breathe a sigh of relief.

Hiding behind locked and secret doors has been the fate of many political and religious groups throughout history. During wartime, those "on the run" in enemy territory have sheltered behind locked doors and in hidden places, and today throughout the world there are many behind locked doors in fear of those who seek to destroy them because of the faith they hold. As I share so openly in worship and witness in my country, I thank God each time I do so for the freedom I possess, for being able to declare my faith openly, without fear. I wonder whether those of us in free countries are always aware of our blessings and whether we support enough in prayer those who have to meet behind locked doors in other lands.

Men and women who have known what it is like to have to hide behind locked doors and those whose experience it is today will identify with the close friends of Jesus who met in a house whose "doors . . . were locked for fear of the Jews." They were desperately afraid and bewildered. They had lived through the most awful days in the history of the world. They had seen their hopes dashed, as their leader had been brutally put to death.

Jesus was dead all right. His had been a public, very public, execution. Then his body had been placed in the tomb, and the heavy stone placed across it, finalizing the life and death of Jesus. Yet now that tomb was empty, the stone rolled away—but by whom? Could it have been the authorities, who would not even allow his body to rest in peace and honor? Surely they had done enough to that body—flogged, tormented, and broken. Mary Magdalene had discovered the empty tomb and had come running for Peter and John, and they confirmed what she had said. Later she had arrived with the fantastic story that she had seen Jesus alive and that he had sent a message for them, but who could believe poor Mary? She had gone through so much anguish, it must have turned her brain! Grief can do that to a person.

If only what Mary had told them could have been true! Could it possibly be true? Their hearts hoped, but their heads knew the hard facts. And yet what was the truth? Would it ever be known? What was to become of them all now, they who had shared so much together with Jesus? They had come to love one another; they wanted to stay together, but what was the point? Surely it would be better to go away, back home, to take up the old life again, separately. If they remained together, they probably would face the same fate as Jesus; they would be thought of as a band of freedom fighters. They were conspicuous as a group; separately they could perhaps merge into the background.

Meanwhile there they were behind locked doors—as a group but also as individuals, each one with memories, fears, questions. Every movement, every sound jogged them into an awareness of how much they were in danger, and deep down they feared that they would be dragged away to suffer the same fate as Jesus—a dreadful prospect!

And then, suddenly, Jesus was there—right there with them. No ghost, no figment of their imagination; it was Jesus. He showed them his wounds, and yet he was alive and well—and yes, even more alive than ever. His words "Peace be with you" were both a greeting and a blessing. They had heard him say those words so often; he had promised them peace, and the sight of his wounds showed them the price of peace.

William Temple says this:

> *He shewed both his hands and his side to them.* It was proof of identity; this, however transmuted, was the Body which had hung on the Cross and was laid in the tomb. But the scars are more than this; they are the evidence not only that what they see is the Body of Jesus, but what is the quality for ever of the Body of Him whom they know with ever-deeper understanding as the Christ . . . .
>
> The wounds of Christ are His credentials to the suffering race of [humans].

Yes, it is Jesus. He does give his peace. He also gives a task to be done, with the authority to do it. Jesus breathes on them, and they receive his life—his Spirit. At creation God breathed on man, and man became "a living being" (Gen. 2:7). God's breath brings life to humankind. The "dry bones" of Ezekiel's vision (Ezek. 37) became alive and active when they received the breath of God. And men and women today can become new people; they too can know new life when they receive the life-giving Spirit of God through Jesus.

New life for all! But the old life has to be put off, discarded, so that the new life can flourish. "Repent and believe" was and is the message. Jesus gave his friends the authority to pronounce the forgiveness of sin, not to forgive on their own account but to pronounce God's forgiveness to the penitent.

Perhaps this has been misunderstood by many. The practice of confession and absolution is often wrongly seen as "wiping the slate clean" by one mortal man for another, something a priest does for those who seek a new start; and the question is, "How can this be so, when no one can forgive sins but God alone?" The answer is surely in these words of Jesus to his friends. He gives authority to remind those who do not recognize their sin that they are not forgiven until they honestly and truly admit their sin and their willingness to turn from it.

There are many who feel it is essential to confess their sins in the presence of a priest or minister, to hear the words of absolution, and to receive a blessing. There are those who, knowing their need of forgiveness, seek counsel from a Christian friend who will be able to assure them through God's word in scripture that their sins are forgiven—for Jesus says they are, and his words are trustworthy and true. But no one has to go to a priest, a minister, or a friend to receive that blessed assurance of forgiveness. Anyone can simply ask Jesus, in the quietness of his or her own heart, and know the peace that comes through forgiveness, the new life of the Spirit.

I have found, as many others have, that to be able to go to someone and share my guilt and repentance, to open my heart, and to have that person assure me of God's forgiveness is an enormous relief and a means of blessing. William Barclay puts it like this:

This sentence does not mean that the power to forgive sins was ever entrusted to any [person or persons]; it means that the power to proclaim that forgiveness was so entrusted; along with the power to warn that forgiveness is not open to the impenitent. This sentence lays down the duty of the Church to convey forgiveness to the penitent in heart and to warn the impenitent that they are forfeiting the mercy of God.

For those friends of Jesus behind locked doors, their sadness was turned into joy, their fears dispelled, by this greeting: "Peace be with you." But for one, it was too good to be true. One friend, Thomas, had not been with the others inside that locked room. He, in his grief, had done what many of us do when overcome with sadness; he had gone away to be on his own. He wanted no one but Jesus, and Jesus was dead. Yet no doubt when he had poured out his grief, he then wanted to be with his friends, to comfort and help them, and so he went to them only to be astonished at the change in them.

The friends greeted him excitedly: "We have seen the Lord." They probably thought that Thomas would accept their word and rejoice with them—but not Thomas! He had experienced the depths of despair, had known the vain hope of it all being a nightmare, then the awakening to stark realization when he knew it was not a nightmare; it was terribly true. He recognized too that the mind can play tricks, and sadly he felt that his friends had been deluded. There was only one way Thomas could accept that Jesus was alive, and that was to touch him. Ghosts and figments of the imagination could not be handled, only real people. Of course someone might have impersonated Jesus, but no one could fake those wounds. Thomas had seen the wounds inflicted—they were real, and the real Jesus would still carry them.

Was it possible that the message his friends so excitedly and confidently shared with him could be true? For a week they tried to convince him. For a week nothing happened. They met together again behind the locked doors, the only difference being that Thomas was with them. It must have been a week of argument, of exasperation at times. Could Thomas have caused the others to doubt that previous experience? Did some of them begin to waver? Why were they still locking doors if Jesus had really come to them? If it was true that Jesus had given them peace and authority, why the locked doors again?

Into the locked room comes Jesus once more. Once more he offers the greeting "Peace be with you." And then, to Thomas, the invitation to discover for himself the living Lord Jesus, by touch. Thomas did not take up the invitation; he didn't need to any more. He knew beyond doubt that it was Jesus. And he knew something else—Jesus was not just his friend and leader, not only his Teacher and Master but his Lord and his God. Thomas would never again doubt the risen Lord. He joined the ranks of those who have met personally with Jesus, Lord and God.

For two thousand years since, others, myself included, have met with that same Jesus, have accepted his forgiveness, his offer of new life, his authority, his Godhead. I have not seen him in the flesh as those first friends of his did, but I know him just the same as they did. I have been freed from fear, from sin, from weakness. I am no longer locked in by those things—for I have discovered freedom, as Charles Wesley did and described so graphically in one of his hymns:

> Long my imprisoned spirit lay,
> fast bound in sin and nature's night;
> thine eye diffused a quickening ray;
> I woke, the dungeon flamed with light;
> my chains fell off, my heart was free,
> I rose, went forth, and followed thee.

For me this is the happiness that Jesus promised to those who see him by faith. This promise he has kept and will keep until the day dawns when I, in company with all believers, will see him face to face and enjoy his presence for all eternity.

Chapter 23

Gone fishing

John 21:1-14

U NTIL ABOUT twenty years ago my experience of fishing was restricted to memories of catching minnows in a net in the canal as a youngster and trailing for mackerel on a trip around the bay in the summer. Then our teenage son was hit by the fishing bug in a big way. Over the following years, our home was gradually taken over by fishing gear, books, and manuals, with unmentionables stored in the freezer for bait. He is now one of the country's leading experts on freshwater fishing, his specialty being the carp. He fishes for carp, writes and lectures, edits magazines, and conducts "carp clinics." He is so dedicated and enthusiastic that even I have become quite knowledgeable on the subject, having gone through twenty years of indoctrination on the joys of fishing. I even appear in his books, which is fair, as he does in mine. I tell him we are both in the fishing business: He fishes for carp; I fish for people.

I am glad my son is a fisherman, for he has an exacting and demanding job as a senior legal officer working in the magistrates' court. Fishing helps him to unwind; it is a safety valve, a way for him to "get away from it all." Over the years I have become used to finding a scribbled note, "Gone fishing, love, Julian," and knowing that he will return tired, relaxed, and happy after his time at the lake. Fortunately too he has an understanding girlfriend who recognizes his need to be out with his rods, for fishing is so much part of him.

The friends of Jesus had been through a most traumatic time. After the three hard years "on the road" with him, they had lived through the despair and horror of his death and the ecstasy of meeting him again after his resurrection. They had been commissioned by him for a life of service, sent out into the world to share the good news and to continue his work. Life was changing dramatically for them, almost minute by minute. They must have felt exhausted by the pressures, exhilarated and yet fearful, keyed up, wondering what on earth was going to happen to them next. It was all so new that they could hardly keep pace with the unfolding revelations.

Then maybe things went rather quiet. They were not sure what their next move should be; they had not yet found their feet—the Day of Pentecost was still in the future! They knew Jesus was alive. They had seen him; he had talked with them and given them their marching orders, but what should they be doing now?

Peter makes his mind up and announces he is going fishing! The others seize on his announcement with enthusiasm; it is a good idea and they will go with him. So off they go on a fishing trip, just like the old days. Why did Peter suddenly decide to go fishing? Perhaps because, like my son when he has a lot on his mind and everything crowding in on him, he sought release in what he enjoyed and knew so well. Peter was a fisherman. Fishing was his trade—it had been his life, and he felt safe and secure doing what he knew he was good at, using the pent-up energy, getting to grips with the old life again.

The others jumped at the chance of getting out in a boat again, hoping to bring back a good catch, for they had to survive by their own means; they were not gentlemen with private incomes but working men—we often forget that. There was no finance committee behind them, no church commissioners sending a salary check at the end of each month—not even a Department of Social Security to help them out! So they set out on the fishing trip. They went at the right time, to the right place, with the right skills, and they caught—nothing.

I can imagine them, tired, dispirited, coming to the conclusion that they were a bunch of failures, wearily making their way back to shore with nothing to show for their night's work. And then someone shouts to them, asks them if they have caught anything. When they shout back, "No," he tells them to try again, fishing this time from the other side of the boat. They respond to the stranger's instructions, to the note of authority in his voice. They do not question his advice; they just get on and follow it. To their delight and amazement, they find their nets full to bursting, so full in fact that they cannot haul them in; probably by this time they were on the point of complete exhaustion.

John looks across, sees the man standing on the shore, and suddenly realizes who it is. "It is the Lord!" he says to Peter. And Peter, impetuous as ever, his tiredness disappearing at the mention of the Lord, jumps into the water, pulling his clothes on so as to be fit to meet his Master. There is work to do first, though; they have to get the catch and the boat to the shore. As they do so, they see that there is a fire burning. Jesus is waiting for them and asks them to bring him some of the fish they have caught.

When everything has been brought to land, the fish counted, the nets inspected and found intact—no breaks in them in spite of the huge catch—Jesus invites the men to eat the breakfast he has made ready. They are afraid to ask who he is, because they really know: It is Jesus who is here with them. And yet it seems so strange meeting him here; they are filled with a sense of awe and wonder. Then, as in the upper room only those few days ago, Jesus hosts the meal with the food prepared by him especially for them.

Why did Jesus choose to meet them in this way, in such a commonplace situation? There they were, a bunch of fishermen returning after a night's fishing with nothing to show for their work. They would not have been expecting to see Jesus, probably not even thinking about anything but keeping their heads down. Yet Jesus was right there, turning their failure to success, providing just what they needed when they needed it.

I expect somehow to meet with Jesus when I am in church, at the big celebrations, as I meditate or read the Bible, or join in prayer with others. I do not really expect to meet him when I have just missed my train connection and the café is closed and I am sitting in a cold, drafty station. He is not uppermost in my thoughts when I am trying to get the car to start, and all I achieve is a dull rattle from the engine as it refuses to fire. Jesus is probably the last person I am thinking about as I frantically hunt for a piece of essential equipment when I am due at an appointment half an hour ago. And yet over and over again, that's just when he does come, does speak, does provide me with what I need—be it patience, comfort, insight, or a clear head. He sets me up again, gives me the encouragement I need to have another go and to get it right— he turns failure into success. I do not mean he waves a magic wand and all the troubles disappear, but he does get right alongside, showing me what really matters, helping me to focus straight again. Very ordinary, practical things—but then he is concerned with ordinary, practical things and with ordinary and often very impractical people!

As Jesus offered the bread and the fish to those hungry and tired friends on the shore of the Sea of Tiberias, the memories of past days must have come flooding back to them. They would have remembered the day Jesus fed the thousands with bread and fish and how they were part of that miracle, distributing the food and clearing up afterward. They would have remembered how he washed their feet before that last supper and how they shared the bread and wine together. As they sat on the shore and munched their breakfast, they probably wouldn't have felt much like talking, just being thankful, enjoying being together with him.

As I come to the Holy Communion service, I am often reminded of past times, of special times, people, and places. Each time I come with open hands to receive, it's a new experience of Jesus and yet a reminder too of previous experiences. There isn't anything I have to say, but, like the friends on the lake shore, I know who it is who feeds me; I know it is the Lord, and I am so very, very thankful.

When Jesus, at the beginning of his ministry, called fishermen to come and follow him, he asked them to leave their old life behind, promising that he would teach them a new trade, catching people. They would be "fishers of people." That promise is to all who respond to Jesus and who choose to follow him. We are all in the fishing business, once we follow Jesus. That's the job he entrusts to us, the task he empowers us to do. Fishing, as the friends found out earlier that night, and as all fishermen know, can be a pretty heartbreaking business. In spite of the effort, the skill, the equipment, sometimes there is nothing to show for all the hard work. Sometimes that experience can go on for a long time— I have seen many dejected, weary fishermen and fisherwomen plodding home empty-handed!

The experience is the same when we are fishing for humankind. We can put so much effort in, use all the right equipment, and still have nothing to show for it. It can go on year after year. I meet ministers and Christian workers who tell me so sadly, "It's all been a waste of time my being in such-and-such a place." Well, it's been said often, but it is worth repeating: We are called to be faithful, not necessarily successful. But failure does hurt!

Perhaps it is only as we lift our eyes from the failure, from our own feelings, our own frustration, that we will see someone in the distance making preparation for us, and we will know it is the Lord! It may be a long haul to the shore, but he will be there. He will be preparing for us; he will welcome us home. And it could be that we will find, to our surprise and joy, quite a catch in our net. One thing is sure: We will have everything we need when we sit down with our Lord in the kingdom of heaven.

Chapter 24 ⟶

A new start in life
John 21:15-24

I T WAS AN ordinary scene, so very ordinary that you would not
have given it a second glance. A boat pulled clear of the water,
nets and catch ready for stowing away, and a group of fishermen
lounging on the shore eating their breakfast, relaxing after a night's
fishing before setting off home or to market. A fire burning, the
smell of cooked fish wafting across the shore, the low sound of
voices. It was a commonplace scene along the shore of the lake. Two
men were slightly detached from the group and were in earnest
conversation, perhaps discussing market prices or whether to get
a new boat. Or maybe it was something far more important than
business transactions, for there was an intense sort of look about
them; you could say they seemed to be "out of this world."

The place is the shore of the Sea of Tiberias, and Jesus, the
risen Jesus, is talking with Peter. This is the first time Jesus and
Peter have met in a "one-to-one" situation since Jesus was arrested,
before he was put to death. Peter had been with the others when
he had come to them in the upper room, but he had just been one
of a group; now Jesus wants to talk to Peter on his own. He has a
great deal to say to him, but first a very searching question: "Do you
love me more than these?"

What a question! In the old days Peter would have flared up,
reading into the words doubt about the superiority of his love.
After all, he had always been first off the mark, the first one to
declare passionately his love and commitment, but he had recently
been proved sadly lacking. When challenged, he had denied he
even knew Jesus. He was the one who looked back to the old life,
who had "taken to the boats" again. It was a very chastened Peter

who replied, "Yes, Lord; you know that I love you." How could he dare to say that his love was stronger than anyone else's? Not now.

You can interpret the question "Do you love me more than these?" as asking, Do you love me more than the old life?—more than being with your friends, more than being the "boss" of the outfit? However you read it, it is clear that Jesus is asking Peter if he puts Jesus first in his life. Jesus asks him the question again— and then again for the third time. Poor Peter! He must have felt so awful remembering that he had actually denied Jesus three times, as Jesus had said he would. Now Jesus is digging into his heart, his will, his whole being. Dare he say he loves Jesus after what he has done? Can the old relationship of trust ever be restored? Does Jesus really believe him? At first, the original Greek makes clear, Peter dares only to reply that he loves Jesus as a friend. He cannot bring himself to claim to have that self-denying, total love that he once claimed—not because he does not feel it but because he knows he did not attain it; he failed Jesus. His professed love was overcome by fear.

The second time Peter is asked, he can again only offer the love of a friend, but then Jesus comes down to his level, it seems, and asks him if he is only his friend. Peter can hardly reply, he is so full of sorrow, remorse, self-doubt. "Lord, you know everything; you know that I love you." The halting words from Peter's lips are of friendship, because he knows his past failures; his heart shouts his love in spite of them.

Jesus knew Peter all right. He knew his love, and because he knew that love was real, he gave Peter the chance to declare it again. Much has been said and written concerning the threefold question, and it does seem that Jesus was giving Peter the chance to wipe out the past. Three times he had denied his Lord; three times he now affirms his love and knows he is accepted. He has a new start, a new chance to prove his love.

How many times do you fail to live up to what you profess? I know I fail so often. It is easy to be bold when things are going well, easy when there is no opposition and we are riding along on the wave of success, ours or others', to profess our one hundred percent dedication and love. It is often a different story when we

are really pushed, when things go against us, when we are seemingly out of our depth; then we find ourselves going back on what
we said with such fervor. Circumstances very often alter cases!
Afterward we could kick ourselves, we feel so ashamed—we, who
thought we were so strong, have proved to be the weak link. Then
it is easy to accept defeat, accept ourselves as failures, and so give
up—in effect, to go back to how things were before, as Peter did,
to the old life. Yet Jesus knows our hearts. He knows whether our
love is real or not. He knows our intention. He knows and under-
stands and gives us another chance—and another and another! I
have heard him speak those words to me after my failures: "Margaret, do you love me?" I can only say with Peter, "Lord, you know
everything . . . ."

As a self-confident teenager, I committed my life to the service of Jesus Christ. I promised my undying love. I would go any-
where, do anything; I would and I could! Three years later I had
turned tail and sought pastures new—a better career, easier life,
good money, more time for myself. It was as a forty-year-old
mother of two that I was again to hear the call to commitment, to
love and to serve. As they say, "a lot of water had flowed under a
lot of bridges." I was older. I knew myself a bit better. I did not so
easily make declarations of undying love! Yet, as to Peter on the
shore, came that insistent "Do you love me more than these, than
all this?" I could only say, "Yes, the Lord being my helper"—and he
has been. He has enabled me to express, at least in some measure,
a degree of love and commitment. It is not one hundred percent,
I confess, but he and I are working on it together!

Peter found when he again said, "I love you" that he was given
a job to do for the one whom he claimed to love. He was to look
after the lambs and the sheep, to care for them and to build them
up—lambs and sheep of the human variety, who are much more
difficult than any of the woolly-backed baa-ing sort!

For me too came the call to look after "lambs" and "sheep."
Sometimes I admit I would prefer those four-legged ones to the
recalcitrant, wayward, obstinate and yet so loving and affection-
ate human ones I am called to care for, who take up so much time,
who make so many demands, and who in the end often wander

off and do their own thing! Yet as I look back on my life, I am so grateful to many who had heard the words of Jesus to "Feed my lambs . . . . Tend my sheep" and who cared for me from the frisky lamb stage right through to the "so set in her ways" sheep! I am thankful for those who still persevere with me—I am sure that, had I been a sheep, I would have been consigned to the meat pie factory long ago!

Being an undershepherd is the most rewarding and exciting life. Seeing the lambs grow up, the flock increase—no, I wouldn't exchange my life for any other! Who knows what may happen in the future, what demands the ministry will make upon me? There may come a time when I am forced into a situation I just don't want to be in, but then that is the risk I have to take, just as every other minister has had to take it since Peter was warned of the cost of being a shepherd.

Peter is forgiven for the past and recommissioned for the future, as Jesus says again those words "Follow me." It is to an older, wiser Peter that the call comes now. He has had to learn the hard way what following Jesus is all about, yet what experiences he has shared in, witnessed for himself; what unique privileges he has enjoyed! Now the call comes again, and he sets off to follow his calling, even to the death. But first there comes a moment when he looks behind him and sees John, "the disciple whom Jesus loved." Does a flicker of resentment or envy pass through Peter's mind as he remembers how special John has always been to Jesus, as he asks, "Lord, what about him?"—a touch of the old Peter!

Jesus firmly replies to Peter's question by telling him to mind his own business! What John or anyone else had to do, where anyone had to go, the end a person would meet, was between the individual concerned and Jesus, not anyone else. Peter had his instructions; he was to get on with following them. Whether John lived a long or short time, whether he would still be around when Jesus returned again—that was not Peter's or anyone else's concern. Of course there were those who misinterpreted the words of Jesus, who read into them something that was not there, but hasn't it always been so! Death came sooner to one and later to the other, but who is to say who had the greater ministry?

Peter, who died a violent death like his Master's, or John, who lived on into old age in exile?

In spite of hearing the words "Follow me" and setting out willingly to do so, I suppose we all glance over our shoulder at times to see what "the others" are up to! "What about him? What about her?" we all want to know, don't we? I know I do! As I pose that question to Jesus, he gives me a tug: "Come on, this way, never mind about anyone else!" I obey—for a while and then ask the same question—and get the same answer!

So I follow on, sometimes rushing and jumping, eager and confident. At other times I drag my feet, dig my heels in, look backwards, but I keep hearing those words: "Follow me!" and when I hear them, I know who is calling. I know his voice. I know that he loves me, that he is my "good shepherd." And so I go on answering: "I'm coming, I'm on my way. Don't let me go, will you?"—and I know for sure that he will never let me go, never let me down, and never let me off the path he has set for me. And what a relief it is to know that!

> O Jesus, thou hast promised
>   to all who follow thee
> that where thou art in glory
>   there shall thy servant be.
> And Jesus, I have promised
>   to serve thee to the end;
> O give me grace to follow,
>   my Master and my Friend.

—John E. Bode (1816–74)

Epilogue ⟶

So where does that leave you?
John 20:30-31; 21:25

WHY DID JOHN write this account of the life and death of Jesus? Why did he record events, relationships, conversations, the lives of so many people? Why did he give such minute details, almost "asides," when he described the greatest event in history, Jesus' resurrection from the dead? Why did he include some things and leave out others? After all, he gives us only a thumbnail sketch. Jesus must have said and done literally thousands of things more than have been recorded by John or any of the other Gospel writers.

John gives the answer quite clearly:

> Now Jesus did many other signs in the presence of his disciples, which are not written in this book. But these are written so that you may come to believe that Jesus is the Messiah, the Son of God, and that through believing you may have life in his name. (John 20:30-31)

So never mind what has not been put down; there is no need to worry about that which we do not possess. In John's account is all we need to know Jesus for ourselves, to realize just who he is, what he has done, and what he offers. There is enough here for anyone!

You could ask why I have been bold enough to try to explain and put into contemporary language what John was talking about in the last eleven chapters of his Gospel account. After all, Margaret Cundiff is no theologian—she possesses the minimum of qualifications; she gained no glittering prizes for academic excellence; she is a very ordinary, middle-aged woman, living in a very ordinary, middle-aged situation. Two thousand years separate her from the things she describes. Yet do they?

I have found these chapters of John's Gospel completely relevant to my life today. It has been as though I had been grasped by the scruff of the neck and made to watch, listen, and be part of the scene. Not as an idle spectator, but as someone who must respond by taking either the way of life or the way of death.

The words of John's Gospel are beautiful, but the danger is that they can become just beautiful, well-known prose, so familiar that the words run off the tongue and away, without ever touching our lives. I have tried to stand with them, to be part of them, to respond to them. As I have done this, I have found myself challenged over and over again by my own lifestyle, by my sometimes secondhand views. I have also seen how my own personal life experiences are part and parcel of my attitude to Jesus. Sometimes these experiences and feelings have had to be broken by him so that I might receive the living bread and not yesterday's stale crusts.

John ends the Gospel account with these words: "But there are also many other things that Jesus did; if every one of them were written down, I suppose that the world itself could not contain the books that would be written." Jesus has gone on doing things since John finished his Gospel account—wonderful things, breathtaking, glorious things: changing people's lives; transforming situations; bringing comfort, hope, strength, and new life in situations and places from one end of the earth to the other. John was right: The world could not contain all the books that would be needed to record the doings of Jesus, for he is still doing them!

This book is my book—you could call it "the good news according to Margaret Cundiff"—and I tell you this, it is all true!

So where does that leave you?

Only you can answer that question. But my advice is that you take up the challenge of Jesus as he says to you today, right now: "Follow me."